THE HEART OF YOUR MONEY

A WOMAN'S GUIDE

How to Create Your Family Financial Values System and Take Control of Your Money

Zena Amundsen, CDFA, CFP, CCS

The Heart of Your Money

First Published in Canada Apr, 2017 by Astra Financial Services
ISBN: 9780995966604

Editor: Nina Shoroplova
Book Cover Design: Greg Salisbury
Typeset: Greg Salisbury
Portrait Photographer: Greg Huszar

DISCLAIMER: This book is a guide intended to offer information on how to become financially independent as a woman. It is not intended in any way to replace other professional advice, but to support it. Readers of this publication agree that neither Zena Amundsen nor her publisher will be held responsible or liable for damages that may be alleged or resulting directly or indirectly from the reading of this publication. This is a work of non-fiction, yet some names have been changed to protect identities.

For my daughters, Mikayla and Isabelle.
You inspire strength, power, courage.

"There are only two ways to live your life. One is as though nothing is a miracle. The other is as though everything is a miracle."

Albert Einstein

Testimonials

"Money isn't about math. **The Heart of Your Money** *is written by a financial professional who actually practices what she preaches. This book is full of practical ideas, stories, and tips that will awaken your financial power!"*

Stephanie Holmes-Winton
CEO, The Money Finder

"Zena Amundsen's book **The Heart of Your Money: A Woman's Guide—How to Create Your Family Financial Values System and Take Control of Your Money** *is a must-read if you are ready to take the bull by the horns and take charge of your money and your financial life.*

"This book is filled with solid content, practical how-tos, and many of the author's rich personal stories that are uplifting and inspiring. All the way through you will say to yourself, 'Wowee, If she can do that, I can too!'

"If you buy one self-help book this year, make it THIS one."

Jackie Black, PhD, BCC
Author of ***Couples and Money: Cracking the Code to Ending the #1 Conflict in Marriage***

"I am inspired that Zena has written a book about money that truly comes 'from the heart.' She has addressed head-on emotional topics and behaviors that are so often avoided and thereby cause so many problems with personal finance. **The Heart of Your Money** *is an important contribution to understanding how to achieve personal financial success.*

"This book will not only inspire and empower women, but anyone who chooses to examine their own relationship to money. Bravo, Zena!"

Rod Tyler, RFP, CFP, CLU
Founder of The Tyler Group

Contents

Contents

Acknowledgements

I need to say thank you and acknowledge many people.

My family has supported me every step of this journey. Ian, you have been a strong advocate, full of love, encouragement, and partnership. I need to acknowledge my parents Jim and Allie and also my in-laws Blair and Nancy.

Throughout my journey, at different times, strong women have appeared to help guide me and offer encouragement. Some encounters were brief and fleeting and I may not put your name to paper but I remember and I carry your wisdom with me.

Here are the ones whose names I can put to paper:

Lora Morrison because you gave me my first job back into the workforce when I needed it the most. You inspired and supported me to find direction. Suzi Volk, for always being there, unconditional love, thirty years of friendship, and much more, for helping to pick me up off the kitchen floor. Sheri Lerat, loving friendship and also helping to pick me up. Linda George, my confidante, for your overwhelming love, support, and contribution. Kristina Jackson for keeping me organized and on track daily. You bring strength to Astra Financial. My Women Wine and Wealth cohorts inspire and energize me. Tina, Lynn, and Kim, the most loving group of women I could ask for. Also, Janet Lee. When I gave you the unedited rough manuscript to read I was full of terror and nerves, but you gave me the assurance that I needed. Jodi Sartison, where would I be without our sanity runs and our friendship?

Rod Tyler, you have been an inspiration and I am grateful to have had you as my mentor. Thank you for the opportunity, encouragement, and skills you gave me so that I could be where I am today. Not only have I learned the expertise of our profession, but I have learned the integrity and love you bring to business and family. Also a thank you to the team at The Tyler Group for your friendship and support. Cheryl Bauer Hyde, I am appreciative of your expertise and willingness to share your knowledge. Thank you for the guidance and friendship.

This book would not have happened without Julie Salisbury at Influence Publishing. I sent you my rough few pages of an idea and you encouraged me and motivated me, trusting me that I could finish this book. Your coaching and guidance has been invaluable. And a special thank you to Nina Shoroplova for your expert editing and patience with me.

Finally, to the Astra tribe, my clients, thank you for your support and trust. Because of you, I get to do what I love every day.

Introduction

Have you ever experienced a turning point in your life? The moment when you knew that the course of your life was changing and you would either stay stuck or move forward?

Wakeup calls force us to come to terms with everything in our life.

Just such a moment left me lying curled up on the kitchen floor, unable to move or breathe, just muttering nonsensically, "How am I going to support my girls?" I was eventually able to peel myself off the floor and function through a three-month daze, still muttering the same thing. I was shell shocked.

I met my husband Ian when I was twenty-one. We were engaged and married six months later with a baby on the way. Money was always short, but love and naivety (okay, *stupidity*) blinded us to the fact that we were poor.

I remember writing a university final exam on our first baby's due date. I was the only nine-month pregnant student trying hard to wriggle out of her desk in the quiet gym while three hundred other students wrote their exam.

That would be my last university class for quite some time. I stayed home to raise our daughters—my second pregnancy came soon after—while my husband pursued his career and supported us. We were broke but in love.

All that came crashing down when he left.

How was I going to support my two young daughters after a marriage breakdown? I had always planned to go back to university and start a career, but this life-changing moment was being forced on me at a time when I was not prepared for it. I had no financial stability. I needed to be responsible for my money. I needed to embrace uncertainty and take back some sort of power for myself. To start, I just needed plain old guts to get off the kitchen floor, get out of my daze, and get on with figuring out how I was going to live.

At the time, it felt like my world was collapsing, but in hindsight it was just the beginning of an awakening force.

I picked myself up, found full-time employment, finished university, created a career, and found a passion. It has been more than ten years since that day on the kitchen floor.

My first job after my husband and I separated was at the head office of a mutual funds company. It was far from glamorous. I worked in the musty basement of an old house that had been converted into offices. My tasks were to scan and file documents. A few months after that I was promoted and eventually I worked my way into client services. Not long after that, I found my mentor and my work home at an independently owned financial planning firm. I completed university and all of my financial planning certifications. My mentor became a friend who helped me, guided me, and cheered me on, but most of all I found myself. I developed confidence and self-sufficiency. This journey helped save my marriage and after almost two years of separation, my husband and I reconciled.

Even so, I decided to continue to control my own destiny. At the end of the day, working for someone else did not leave me feeling in control. Like many other women, I was busy making money for a male-dominated company, helping push someone else up the mountain to their success. I needed to ensure that I was steering my life and stepping into my own power—the power of controlling my career, my finances, my wealth, and my future. It was vital that I recognize and harness my value, worth, and potential for my own gain.

I remember the moment that I looked down at my suit and realized that I was wearing the same gender-neutral grey suit as my sixty-five-plus male peer. Why did I feel the need to replicate, fit in, blend in, and not be different? It was then I started my own financial planning company.

Leaving that firm and creating my own company was not easy. I left something familiar and safe to go on to something new and unknown. But, throughout every step of my journey and story, I have learned the power of self-confidence and support. I have found strength in listening and sharing stories with other women. We women all share a commonality of having to fight to recognize our own worth and strength.

My story is a common one. We are steering the course of change in our own lives and in the lives of the people in our family. We women are earning more, becoming better educated, and demanding more control and power in our lives. We are choosing the responsibility to lead our family to financial success by organizing and overseeing our family money.

Nurturing our connection with money and being financially literate helps ground us, gives us a sense of peace and ease, and allows us to kick-ass in the other areas of our lives.

The old way of financial planning and advice is on the way out the door. You know, the salesman, the sales pitch of buying a product, the magic formula that will make you rich. The only prescription that works is not magic, but it is achievable—create a healthy, honest relationship with your money, and become informed. I am going to share with you the power of abundance and how to find the right advice that is in your best interest and not just a sales pitch meant to make the salesman a large fat commission.

Throughout this book, you will learn my story and be invited to look deeply at your own story and how it reflects in your money world today. These pages are meant to bring you confidence and knowledge so that you may create your own destiny filled with prosperity and success.

I wrote this book—*The Heart of Your Money*—with the hope that women in all stages and all walks of life will talk about and feel comfortable with their money. I want women to feel self-assured, less stressed, and—even more importantly—motivated to take control of their money. I want you to make your money work for you.

I invite you to join the journey. Reclaim the heart of your money.

Chapter 1—Confidence

"The time will pass anyway. You can either spend it creating the life you want or spend it living the life you don't want. The choice is yours."
Unknown

Most often the couples who come through my office door looking for financial advice and planning are led by women. The couple is collaborating through a team effort, but the woman's distinct drive stands out. The motivation goes beyond accumulating mass wealth and returns. She is driven by trying to understand the complicated system so that she can feel informed, in control, confident, and powerful.

My drive came from a place of vulnerability. I was left exposed and financially naked. Not all women whom I meet have this same story, but they do have the same sense of vulnerability that they want to kick to the curb. In fact, the women I meet are taking the lead to ensure that they will be okay no matter what—crisis or no crisis. They have a determined desire to take on the responsibility of managing their family's finances and they don't need an excuse or gut-wrenching story to do so.

According to Statistics Canada, women who work full-time in Canada still earn 73.5 cents for every dollar men make. The numbers are even lower for women in a minority group. This is reason enough for wanting to take some control of your family's money decisions. Speaking personally, I want to control and mitigate my vulnerability and make sure I use my money to help give me back some sense of power, since I am already starting at a wage-gap deficit when comparing my earning power with that of a man's. I don't want to pass the buck on important money matters.

Women have progressed considerably in terms of education and schooling over the past few decades. Just twenty years ago, a smaller percentage of women than men aged between twenty-five and fifty-four had a post-secondary education. Today, the situation in Canada is completely different. Education indicators show that women generally get higher marks than men. This gap in favour of women is even noticeable at a young age, since girls often get better marks than boys in elementary and secondary school.[1]

In 2008, 62 percent of all university undergraduates in Canada were women. We are also on the rise to be the family breadwinners. A Prudential Research Study found that nearly half of the women who responded to their survey—44 percent—are the primary breadwinners in their households. And 65 percent of those who responded said they take the lead role in financial and retirement planning.[2]

It seems logical that the next step for women is to be the ones who manage our family finances appropriately. Let's face it, we have a lot at stake. We earn less than the average male and we live longer than men. When it comes to saving, this means the earning gap is magnified. We have less disposable income available to save, and every penny counts when we are saving for our family and for retirement. The bag lady syndrome—the fear of ending up penniless and homeless—is real. This fear is deepened by the fact that senior women are more likely to be living alone with a low income.[3]

Michelle is a friend who controls her family finances because she feels she is more financially savvy than her partner. She took on the role of handling every aspect of the finances, from daily spending and paying bills to planning for retirement. "I handle everything and I like it that way. My husband can sometimes be a procrastinator and I want to be assured that our savings are managed appropriately and that our day-to-day is taken care of. I like being the CFO of my house." Michelle is just one of many women who are actively choosing to take a lead.

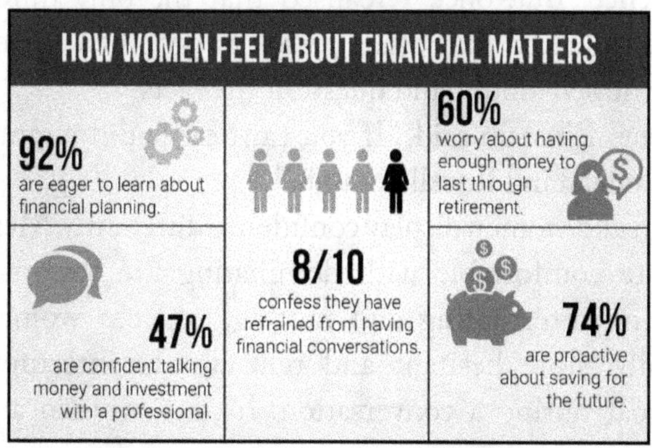

HOW WOMEN FEEL ABOUT FINANCIAL MATTERS
92%
are eager to learn about financial planning.
8/10
confess they have refrained from having financial conversations.
60%
worry about having enough money to last through retirement.
47%
are confident talking money and investment with a professional.
74%
are proactive about saving for the future.

What Holds Women Back from Achieving Financial Equality?

A lack of confidence.

The biggest financial barrier that I see is that we women can be champion self-doubters. Even in my financial profession and on my own journey of gaining my personal money power, I have to turn off the inner voices of self-doubt. I know that I am intelligent, educated, and very capable, but every once in a while, the gremlins take over my confidence. I am often at professional events attended mostly by men with the exception of maybe just a couple of women, including myself. The male-dominated financial world is fantastic at creating a false barrier of exclusiveness and intelligence by using obtrusive language and jargon. There is a sense of pride in being able to baffle with bullshit. I will admit that my insecurity kicks in, I feel very unsure of myself, and I question my confidence. I mean, if "he" is talking down to me and using these large complicated charts and equations, he must be smarter than me, right? WRONG! For those short few moments, I lacked confidence. But, once I realised that the only difference between me and that other person is ego, then I can shut down the self-doubt and question the facts.

Albert Einstein said, "If you can't explain it simply, you don't understand it well enough."

Men and women display confidence differently. Men may be more comfortable with dominating the conversation, including interrupting and ranting, whereas women are generally more hesitant and reluctant to interrupt and showboat during a conversation. In fact, women are less likely to respond and answer a question in a group setting for fear of bringing attention to themselves.

One of the challenges of the financial industry that I see is that it is predominantly run by men. The typical male financial advisor is not helping women's confidence factor. Inevitably, the financial world is comprised of men advising men. Men tend to approach life issues quite differently than the way women do. Many women feel that since they do not know the language or the terms, they can't ask questions; they worry their questions will sound dumb. In my experience, women are starving for more information but not getting what they need even when seeking it out.

I met with Tracy, a brilliant corporate manager, who shared with me her experience with a male financial advisor. Tracy is a very well-educated woman who manages a staff of ten and makes important business decisions every day on short notice. She is a force to be reckoned with. She explained to me that she assumed her first meeting with the advisor would just be a chat over a cup of coffee, so they could get to know each other. She shared that during coffee, she quickly felt confused and bulldozed all at the same time. He was pushy and demanding with a sense of urgency. I was shocked when she told me that because she didn't know what to do, she just signed the paperwork and transferred her accounts over to him. Tracy was embarrassed while she explained this. Her gut reaction at the time had been telling her to run, but her fear and lack of knowledge left her stunned in that moment. Her uneasiness around her money only increased. It took her six years to muster up the courage to make a change and demand better service and more knowledge from an advisor who truly has her best interests at heart—me; it also cost her six years of low investment returns.

Katty Kay and Claire Shipman, the authors of *The Confidence Code : The Science and Art of Self-Assurance—What Women Should Know*, write about the science and art of confidence, and the shortage of female confidence. They found that on averages based on numerous worldwide studies, women effectively believe they are 20 percent less valuable than men believe they are. I share this because our confidence and our money align harmoniously with our internal well-being and sense of fulfillment. Without sureness or certainty, we can't achieve the peace of mind or ease necessary for successful financial decision-making.

What Is Confidence?

It is hard to pinpoint the definition of confidence, because it means something different to each individual. Authors Kay and Shipman share their definition in an article they wrote: "Confidence is not, as we once believed, just feeling good about yourself. If women simply needed a few words of reassurance, they'd have commandeered the corner office long ago. Perhaps the clearest, and most useful, definition of confidence we came across was the one supplied by Richard Petty, a psychology professor at Ohio State University, who has spent decades focused on the subject. 'Confidence,' he told us, 'is the stuff that turns thoughts into action.'"[4]

Confident women are changing the world and changing their financial outcome.

Male versus Female Styles of Investing

Financial institutions and researchers have long studied gender differences regarding investing. Over the years it has been confirmed that men enjoy learning on their own and are generally more confident about investing. Women on the other hand are more goal-orientated and prefer learning in a group setting. Behavioural finances psychology has taught us that women are less confident with their financial decisions. This doesn't have to be a hindrance. Please don't read this and feel that you should interpret it to mean you are unqualified. Let's flip this to mean that you have the potential to be powerful with your quest for assurance and information.

Women are more likely to seek professional advice, which is a huge benefit. All you have to do is think of the old cliché of a man not asking for directions and ending up getting lost. You have the ability to seek direction and get to where you want to go faster and with more ease. What if the assumption, "I do not know enough" were the key to financial success? What if recognizing that there is a need to learn more were the smartest decision a woman could make?

What Does Financial Empowerment Look Like?

There is no correct answer to this question. Your answer will be different from everyone else's.

I believe all women should be claiming their financial power. It does not matter how much money you make.

You are in charge. You control your destiny and you make decisions based on what is right for you. True wealth and happiness create a life that is aligned with your unique values and dreams, the ones coming from your heart. Claiming your financial power is not about stockpiling money. It is about understanding how your money and your heart work together; it is about using money to live your life, on your own individual terms.

I interviewed a number of women in an attempt to better understand how women can create financial confidence and learn what financial empowerment looks like to them. We can learn, relate, and help form our own vision of power by reading each woman's definition of financial empowerment. Two of the common themes I found among their answers are freedom and choices.

It Looks Like Independence, Freedom, and Security to Betty

> "It might be true that 'money can't buy happiness,' but it can gain you independence, freedom, and security. Financial empowerment looks like being the driver of my own destiny, having some immunity from outside forces, and security for the 'what ifs' to me."

It Looks Like Freedom and Control to Brenda

> "To me, financial empowerment is the ending phase of a long line of life choices, of getting myself to a place where I can enjoy the freedoms of retirement and of life finally slowing down! Beginning back in high school, financial

empowerment meant making choices that would leave all doors open for me so I could attend university to give myself the education I would need to find a job that would be satisfying and allow me to live comfortably. It meant marrying a spouse who held the same beliefs, values, and end goals for our life as mine. Right now, with two very busy teens, financial empowerment means being able to provide for our children. Being able to allow them to join activities and clubs and perform competitively in their chosen activities. Having control over where we would like our investments and money to go. Not having to worry week-to-week about finances."

It Looks Like Being in Charge of Her Financial Security to Jennifer

"Financial empowerment to me is being in charge of my financial security.

"I'm the one in charge of sticking to my cash flow plan and saving for vacations, car and home repairs, and of course retirement!

"I am the only one solely responsible for being accountable if the numbers don't add up. Sometimes it's overwhelming but knowing I have a plan makes it an exciting challenge.

"Call me crazy ... but I love being in charge of my financial future!"

It Looks Like Making Choices to Kim

"When I was growing up, both my parents worked outside the home to raise me and my two sisters. They didn't have 'glamorous' jobs or large paycheques, nor the choice to stay at home or choose between a vast number of jobs in our small rural community. They worked hard, at respected professions—mechanic and shop owner; waitress and restaurant manager, then later, bank teller. Both had opportunities to move into management jobs but never wanted the headaches that they felt went with them.

"Among many things, I learned from them how to work hard; how to treat others with respect no matter their job, their choices, or their 'lot' in life; and how to be proud of the life you make for yourself.

"So, I think for me, financial empowerment starts with that and is maybe that simple: to work and do what is necessary to make the life that I choose for myself and for the people that I call my family. By 'family,' I'm referring to others regardless of whether they are family by the typical definition (spouse, children, aging parents), or by the broader, more holistic definition (partners, colleagues, friends, community, etc.).

"Years ago, financial empowerment meant having enough money in the bank and being 'smart' and budgeting enough to have just my husband work so that I could stay home; later it meant working part-time while our kids were young. Later still, financial empowerment meant my husband working part-time and me working full time while he worked on finishing his PhD. Later yet, it meant I quit my full-time job and bought a coffee shop and now both of us are self-employed entrepreneurs.

"Financial empowerment at its simplest is the ability for me to make choices—whatever choices are right for me and my family, balanced with contributing to my community.

Right now that 'contribution' is more one of my time and abilities. Later on in life, it will probably tend to be more in the financial areas.

"I truly believe and have long told my kids (and, well, whomever else will listen!) to be proud of whatever life they choose to make for themselves—to be good people, to be kind and respectful to others, and to 'lift others up.' Whatever job you do and however much money you make, whether you are a billionaire or a waitress, do your job well and be happy at it; or make a change to do another job that fits you better. Make sure you can support yourself and your family, and hold your head high. So I think that is my financial empowerment."

It Looks Like Money Moving Constantly to Ann

"Financial empowerment looks like money moving constantly. Creating, making, buying, selling, spending, improving, saving, learning, applying, trying, persevering, earning. Following your dream. Actually, putting into place those ideas, thoughts, and dreams that seem so unattainable. One step at a time. Follow that nagging feeling that nudges you in a certain direction. Learn what you need to learn and be empowered by your mistakes.

"Financial empowerment to me is being responsible when you need to be, and then indulging because you can. Feeling good about money. Actually FEELING GOOD about money. Not worrying about where it will come from but trusting that it will show up. Not feeling guilty about having money, and not feeling like I have to spend it just because I can.

"Money is not a financial status symbol for me. It's my own little secret with myself. My mind is wealthy, no one needs to know this, it's my personal relationship—it's none of your business. My money is not there to flaunt, because then I'm making it your business. It's my quiet, subtle relationship that I nurture and tend to. In turn, my money reciprocates and matches what I put into our relationship.

"Financial empowerment looks like just knowing the money is there when I need it, and that more will show up when I spend what I have. It looks like not ever really being satisfied—not in a greedy way, but in a constant, self-assessment, self-improving way. Never thinking that I have reached my peak; realizing that there is always room to grow and teach and inspire. It is empowering to know and believe that there is no limit to the greatness that can come into your life when you expect it to. Money included. It is there to make my life great. I expect it to and therefore it will. It is a mental state that took me years to wrap myself in, but I have never looked back. I don't need to, because whatever I expect, I create. It almost feels like magic how accurate it is. It's the universe at work. It's wonderfully empowering."

It Looks Like Breaking Free of Old Belief Patterns to Jivi

"As a woman, financial freedom to me means to have broken free of old belief patterns that were ingrained in me and that limited my self-confidence about financial abundance. These models of construct came from hearing comments such as, 'You don't know how to handle money';

'You make decisions with your heart': 'You don't think about the pros and cons when you purchase something'; 'If you make the wrong decision you are taking away from your children's future'; 'You are too naive and people will take advantage of you'; and the best of all, 'You are just too nice and you make emotional decisions.'

"All these comments solidified over many years that my financial success was dependent on having a male figure in my life. To be frank, it was also easier to allow my ex-husband to handle the finances, because it meant I did not have to be responsible for the financial results.

"When I look back, it was not that I lacked the intelligence to learn; it was that I was making a choice to stay oblivious so that I did not have to be accountable for our financial situation. I would start to learn a little and then as soon as the realization became clearer that I would have to control my spending, I would pretend to get frustrated and say, 'I just can't do this, it's just not who I am or how I think.' This excuse was much easier than accepting the truth that I did not want to budget my finances. My ex-husband handling the finances was also a wonderful safety blanket that I could hide under and pretend everything was going to be okay.

"That easy ride quickly changed when I got divorced about seven years ago and found myself regretting not being involved in our finances. Coming from a twenty-year relationship in which my ex-husband had always handled the money, I faced the greatest fear of my life—I had to learn about finances. I had grown up not being very good in math; I had actually managed to avoid it most of my education and career. Not being good in math for me equaled not knowing how to handle money.

"Then, there I was at forty-four years of age having to learn a new life skill that I wished I had learned early on. I lacked self-confidence, self-worth, and felt stupid even asking someone for help. What was I going to say—that I was in a highly intellectual career and yet had no concept of how to handle my finances? My greatest fears manifested in thoughts such as, 'What if I can't pay my rent? What if I forget to pay a bill? How will I be able to afford my living standard?'

"It's important to provide some context here, that I was making well over a six-figure income in a government job. Hence most of my expenses such as healthcare, travel expenses, etc. were covered. From a perspective of pure reality, there was no reason to worry about money.

"But, due to my low self-confidence, it had become my greatest fear that I would somehow fail with money. I had to talk to someone to get out of this victim mentality, so I reached out to my good friend and disclosed to her that I had never gone into a bank; I had never paid a utility bill; I had never even looked at investments; and I had no idea about savings. I remember sitting on the couch sharing this with her with my eyes filled with tears in complete vulnerability, wondering whether she was judging me.

"She looked at me with compassion and empathy and said to me, 'Don't worry. We can learn all that; it's very easy.'

"I remember her pulling out a calculator and asking, 'How much do you make per month and how much is your rent?' Just from the answers to those two questions, she showed me that I had a surplus of $4,000 each month. What I relief. I thought, what was I thinking?

"Years later, she told me that she had felt the most sad for me when I told her about my financial fears and could not really comprehend how someone so intellectual could not possibly know these things. She was sadder for me about that than for my actual move post my divorce and for my having to leave my kids behind. This was all new learning for her and it was all new learning for me.

"This started a journey of understanding the basics of what my incoming finances looked like as well as all my outgoing expenses. Then I started to put together some savings and learn about investments. I would soon come to understand that my money worries were completely unfounded. As my confidence started to build, so did my own self-worth that I could make sound financial decisions.

"Then it was time to make the next step. I hired a money coach who spent the next three months teaching me about budgeting. This opened up a whole new world of knowledge for me that I didn't think was even possible. My bank statements made more sense, I was more comfortable going into a bank and meeting with my financial advisor, and I was starting to have great control over my personal finances. It was time to tackle my business financial situation.

"One very pivotal milestone in my financial learning was when my sister who also happens to be my Chartered General Accountant said to me that I had to terminate all five of the members of my financial team and do the work myself to financially stabilize my business. I spent the next year understanding my business finances including budgeting.

"It was definitely not the best time of my life, but I gained the most valuable learning that year. I learned how much time it takes to do all the tasks in my business so that I would know if I was being overcharged. I learned that it is better to do some tasks myself as they take me less time and less money. That particular year, I learned the value of a dollar and how we must use our conscious awareness in spending every dollar with purposeful intention in the most efficient manner. I started to get three quotes for any service I wanted so that I could compare apples to apples and get the most cost-efficient option for the quality of work. Every decision was made with great intention and awareness that I was spending the dollar at the best place possible. I had spent most of my career teaching mindfulness and here I was learning financial mindfulness. I was learning to be patient with each moment so that I could get the best return on investment, whether I was spending one dollar or a hundred dollars. I was learning that mindful spending meant that I did not purchase something right away; rather I would walk away and see if the need for that particular item came up at least three times before making the purchase. "Financial empowerment does not mean being cheap; however, it does mean being frugal and knowing exactly where your money is being spent. I was no longer afraid to ask questions about what exactly I was getting for the amount I was spending. If I did not get what I had paid for, I was no longer afraid to communicate that I was disappointed and ask for it to be corrected. In the past these types of conversations would be difficult for me and I would simply just leave them. Sometimes, I would even pay another person to do the exact same project without asking the original person to correct it. I started to question each project and its return on investment, wondering what I had in hand after paying for the service. If I could not justify what I would have in my hand, the decision was clear about whether or not I would continue to spend money.

"Now, things are very different. Having understood the value of the dollar as well as contributing to others' economic growth, I am more confident in my financial decisions. Financial empowerment is less about money and more about knowing who you are and having the self-confidence that you can make fiscally responsible decisions. Sometimes these decisions are not easy ones because it may mean that you can't do something that you really desire in that moment in time.

"I am more accountable and responsible for the choices I make because I can no longer rely on my go-to sentence, 'I don't handle the finances so I don't know.' 'I don't know' was no longer good enough. That was an easy cop out so that I did not have to learn about incoming and outgoing money and I didn't have to be responsible for the sometimes-wrong decisions.

"There are so many beliefs that we collect about money when we are growing up, some great and some not so great. It's important to understand what those beliefs are that you have about money and then deconstruct each one to form new ones that leave you in control of your future financial situation. Don't be afraid to be vulnerable and share with someone you trust that you need help; we each learn different life skills at various times due to life circumstances.

"I can say today that I have gained the freedom of feeling in control, liberated from all the limiting beliefs that I had about money, which are no longer true, and I have gained accountability because I am in the driver's seat of my own future. Even though there is much more accountability on my part and I have to take responsibility when things don't go as anticipated, I have never before felt more in control of my financial future.

"There have been three main lessons that I have come to learn:

"There is nothing wrong with making decisions with my heart as long as I remember to take my head with me.

"Financial success is solely based on my conscious awareness of how I make decisions about the best value for my dollar.

"Money is more about self-worthiness, that I can make decisions that result in financial abundance."

Jivi Saran is the author of *Permission to be YOU*. As a Corporate Mentalist she empowers women in CEO and leadership roles to step into their own power and build the immortal legacy of their leadership and business strategy. Connect with her at www.thecorporatementalist.ca or follow her work at www.facebook.com/thecorporatementalist.

Reaching financial empowerment is a journey that can transform your choices into desired opportunities. Having a clear picture of what it means to you to have control over your finances will help you build your self-confidence around money. So, take a moment and ask yourself, What does financial empowerment look like to you?

Chapter 2—Our Past Is Not Our Future

"It is not in the stars to hold our destiny but in ourselves."
Shakespeare, Julius Caesar

It took me until I was thirty-one to realize my own truth with money. It was then that I was forced to look in the mirror and come face to face with everything that was coming to a head—my marriage ending, my children's future, and my own future. The one constant I felt through all of the turmoil was that money had all the power in every scenario. Money has power. Plain and simple. It is the longest relationship we will ever have, from our birth to our death. It is longer than our marriages and our friendships. And sometimes it holds the power in those relationships. That was exactly how I felt at that time. Money had me pinned against the wall.

Have you ever counted how often the thought of money creeps into your brain in a day? The ongoing inner dialogue and conversation in your head that discusses everything from making a grocery list, planning the next vacation, and filling your car with gas, to watching television as it tells you what you need to buy to feel happy. Thoughts swirl with "How much is that going to cost?" "Is there enough?" "Am I doing the right thing with my money?" We don't even realize when the inner chatter pops in.

I caught inner dialogue rambling one day when driving. I noticed a magnificent front yard and flower garden. My thoughts went from beauty and appreciation to referring back to my yard and how much I would enjoy having that. My thoughts went from comparing and planning what I would need to buy to complete the project to how much it would finally cost. That's just an example of thirty seconds out of a day of twenty-four hours.

Our society, our modern consumer world, is overloaded with the concept of money all around us. Even at work, staff meetings, budget meetings, cost analysis.... No wonder our money anxiety is so high. And that is a regular day of inner money chatter that doesn't include the catastrophic event of a marriage breakdown.

I am not saying that having wealth and money *is* power. I am stating that money *has* the power in our life. It is like the evil vampire that gets stronger by sucking more and more blood. If we give the power over to money, it will just continue to suck and suck until we are emotionally and physically dry.

The only way to manage this is to confront it. When we confront money we can turn it into freedom and peace. This is part of the journey, getting to a point when we can turn off negative thoughts, turn off anxiety, and flip to a state of feeling in control and finding a sense of peace, reconciliation, forgiveness, and love.

Chapter 2

A Money Memory Story

Everyone has a money story. What is it? It is your relationship with money. It is all the pain and all the joy blended with some fulfillment into the history of your life. It is your strengths and challenges, your past intersecting with your present. It is vulnerable to confront these memories and put them together.

Becoming familiar with our own unique story means honouring the past, learning from it, and then creating a new story that includes abundance. This process is a powerful tool that will challenge your beliefs and help you transform your present day money story. This is the first step in creating a story that has you in control and feeling positive and powerful. Recognize and move past the feelings that are limiting your prosperity and your happiness.

My first memory with the concept of money is from when I was about four years old. I remember shopping at the Salvation Army. I can still smell the mustiness and visualize the dark, packed racks and shelves of used items. My mom was a struggling, poor single woman and we shopped at the Salvation Army for school clothes and shoes. I knew that we couldn't afford a lot. I knew that Fridays were a treat of fries and gravy at the Tastee-Freez. I thought that the three-foot Christmas tree and the homemade cut-out Christmas cards as decorations were beautiful. But the used shoes from the Salvation Army that didn't fit properly and smelled as though they had decayed has haunted me ever since. I knew that we couldn't afford the brand new light up runners that the other children had. I was embarrassed by my shoes.

My first memory is one of scarcity, meaning I felt like I didn't have enough.

Fast forward thirty-five years:

That memory helps me explain to myself why over the years I have bought too many new shoes that I may never wear. It has only been since coming to terms with my relationship with money that I realize that there is an underlying reason why I have piles of shoes everywhere. I don't necessarily ever wear them. Some still have their price tags and some don't even fit properly. I have finally been able to put together my mindset behind buying them. I now stop and ask myself truly why I am buying another pair of shoes. I ask myself why I feel the need for more. What is the true reason behind this purchase? What hole or void am I trying to fill?

Now, don't get me wrong. I have not cured my shoe problem one hundred percent. I have noticed that every once in a while, a few more pairs of new shoes creep into my closet. I recognize that this correlates with when I am feeling vulnerable and my scarcity mindset slithers around. I have even recognized when I overcompensate with my daughters and try to buy them shoes. Somewhere my money memory of scarcity kicks in and I retaliate without checking in with myself. There is a rap song I heard my teenagers listening to once and it babbled, "Check yourself before you wreck yourself." That is now one of my mantras.

I have learned to connect my memories and money stories with my present self.

When I was eight years old, my mom and I moved in with the person I know as Dad today. We moved to a small town. Life changed drastically for the better. We had a newer car, a new home, stability, and love (and no more used shoes!). Even while I remember this abundance, there is still a cloud of scarcity that pushes through with my memories from this time. I remember my mom commenting that she didn't have enough money or that she would have to use the credit card for certain purchases.

Lying on my kitchen floor in 2005 after my husband had left flooded back every feeling of scarcity in my bones. I could feel what it was like to be poor all over again. I was full of fear and doubt.

No matter how hard we work at having a healthy and abundant relationship with money, there will be trigger points and moments that can set us back. The key is to not catch yourself stuck in insufficiency mode. Abundance can be overshadowed by the actions, conversations, and trigger points that portray scarcity and fear, and the ideas that we sometimes correlate with money and value such as I am not enough, I don't have enough, I need more.

Improving Self-Value and Self-Worth

Can improving our self-value and worth improve our financial situation?

Yes, self-love equals self-care and self-care equals the motivation to nurture our financial health.

Self-love = self-care = motivation

There is a sense of deserving that needs to happen for self-value and self-worth to kick in, because you do deserve an elevated sense of your own worth. Our judgment and our attitude toward what we believe we deserve are linked to our money story and our first memories. If we feel undeserving, we can be our own worst enemy and create roadblocks to improving our financial situation.

For example, I met with a client who had come from a divorced family. Her father left when she was ten and her mother raised her and her brother. My client grew up struggling financially but also emotionally. She shared with me that she felt abandoned and didn't and still doesn't understand why her father has not continued a relationship with her and her brother. She went on to graduate from university with full scholarships, to find stable employment, and then to complete her master's degree while working, all debt free. She now earns more than $150,000 a year. When I met her, she had credit card debt, no savings, and was living from paycheque to paycheque. If she accumulated any amount of cash, she felt she had to get rid of it; she experienced an unsettling feeling—an almost urgent feeling—that it shouldn't be there. She would shop and spend it immediately. Her scarcity mindset and her relationship with self-worth and self-love were causing her to release money she had, because deep down she felt like she didn't deserve it.

Once we went through her history, her money story, and her memory, we could connect her self-value and how she perceived her self-worth and money. Nowadays, she can still spend and not feel restricted, but not until after she has taken care of all her savings buckets and retirement savings she needs in order to protect and love her future self. She can then spend what is left guilt-free from a place of abundance with self-love in mind.

I started my relationship with money because of a marriage breakdown, but all it takes is a mini wakeup call or maybe you just have a long nagging feeling of unease and doubt that stop you from taking back control.

Our money attitudes are financial but mostly emotional. How our parents handled money has a large impact on how we deal with our own money today. Whether we overspend and are in debt or we agonize over our money decisions, save everything, and penny pinch, we can trace back to having either accepted our parents' money beliefs or having rejected their attitudes. Either way we reflect our history into our current money behaviours.

The key is to know and recognize our money-beliefs story, talk about it, honour it, and then separate from it and choose to create our own. Our current money story does not define us today. It is a learning experience that helps us grow.

Money Lessons

Along with our money memories, our money lessons are just as important.

What did your parents teach you about money? Did you talk about money growing up? Were you included in money conversations as children?

I learned about money from my parents, and they learned about it from theirs, and so on.... Whether these were negative or positive money lessons, I inherited the same concepts my family had around finances.

My mom's money lessons were non-existent. She shared with me that her parents taught her that you do not talk about money. It was taboo and rude to bring up politics, religion, and especially money. As an only child, she grew up on military bases. My grandfather was in the air force and they continually moved across Canada. Because Mom's parents were busy socializing and entertaining on these military bases, she was left on her own a lot. Her parents compensated for this lack of time they spent with her by giving her gifts.

My mom shared with me a money lesson that stands out for her. She remembers working hard at odd jobs and saving up for a new bicycle. She had felt proud that she had come up with a savings plan and initiated ways to earn money. When her birthday came along, her parents bought her the bicycle. She reminisced with me that she was so upset and disappointed. She had wanted to pay for the bike herself. Her parents didn't acknowledge that she had been working hard and saving. She felt insignificant, upset, and worthless. This story brought a realization and significance for how she developed her money beliefs, attitudes, and habits.

When she told me this story, I could piece it together with an understanding that is more profound than just saying she is "bad" with money. While we talked about this story, my mom felt that her self-confidence and sense of accomplishment had not been recognized. She believes that this example emphasized that she was not taught to be responsible with money and respect it. There was a disconnect between the power of earning money and respecting it enough to value it. Self-worth and earning money are essential to a healthy relationship with our finances. My mom feels as though she missed out on the life lessons and opportunities that parents can use to teach about money.

Money Shame

The freedictionary.com defines shame as "A painful emotion caused by the awareness of having done something wrong or foolish; a pervasive, negative emotional state, usually originating in childhood, marked by chronic self-reproach and a sense of personal failure; a condition of disgrace or dishonor; ignominy; a regrettable or unfortunate situation, one that brings dishonor, disgrace, or condemnation."

Add at the end of each of these definitions "with money."

Shame is a painful emotion caused by the awareness of having done something wrong or foolish with money.

Shame is a pervasive, negative emotional state, usually originating in childhood, marked by chronic self-reproach and a sense of personal failure with money.

Shame is a condition of disgrace, dishonour, and ignominy with money.

Shame is a regrettable or unfortunate situation to do with money; one that brings dishonour, disgrace, or condemnation.

This is Money Shame.

This sums up how most of us perceive ourselves. I have worked with people who make $30,000 a year and people who make $300,000 a year. The money shame is the same for each.

There are common sayings we might have heard and believed in our families:

- Don't talk about money; it isn't appropriate.
- I am just not good with money.
- She is just not good with money.
- It's just way over my head.

- I am too creative and free-spirited to get a handle on it.
- We don't have two nickels to rub together.
- That's too rich for my blood.
- We can barely make ends meet.
- I should have more in the bank right now.
- Where does it all go?
- It takes money to make money.
- Money is the root of all evil.
- I don't deserve that; it costs way too much.

At some point in our life, we have all heard these sayings. They leave an imprint on us and, in some way, we might believe them. I am guilty of doing so and I recognize myself in most of these. In fact, I am pretty sure I have said them all.

I am pretty sure I told myself in my twenties that not having money was just fine. I didn't want to be materialistic and stuck up because I thought that is what people who make money are. What a limiting belief and a shameful money attitude! Then when reality sank in as a parent and caregiver, I realized that I did need to earn a good living and make money. But then the next money shame sank in and screamed in my ear, "I should have more in the bank right now. I should be earning more. I need more." This shame became the dog chasing his own tail around and around and never catching it.

Money shame shows up in different ways. It can be the dread of opening your bills in the mail; the feeling in the pit of your stomach when you think or talk about money; the envy and self-loathing inner chatter you create. Either way, we are not immune to money shame. It is just a matter of recognition and then self-permission to heal and move on.

I drove the same Toyota station wagon my dad bought me all through high school and the first few years of marriage until 1999. My plan was to keep driving it until it stopped. But with my second baby on the way, my dad surprised us with a newer-to-us 1991 Toyota Previa minivan. What a treat! My oldest daughter no longer needed to cram next to our 130-pound Rottweiler and continually jam her fingers and toes into his mouth. He was a great dog, but still!

That van lasted us until we sold it for an upgrade in 2007. I can't tell you the happy dance I did when we had automatic windows and air conditioning. I had one smaller inexpensive, great-on-gas car after that.

Right now I drive a small Mercedes. I planned and saved for the expense and considered the purchase carefully beforehand. I did all of the right things financially. I practised what I preached. But … it took me three to four months to feel comfortable driving it.

If friends commented "Nice car," I would immediately be embarrassed and downplay it, saying we had bought it at a great price. I would make excuses for why I got it instead of a cheaper model. "You know it was an end-of-year sale." "They took twenty thousand off the asking price." I went on and on.

I had and still have money shame. Why? What belief is holding me back? Why am I embarrassed?

I worried about calling my parents and telling them what I had bought with fear of some judgment or them not agreeing with my purchase. I put off the phone call. I think the belief I had was "I don't deserve that; it costs too much." Why don't I deserve that? We live a very modest, simple life without very many possessions or unnecessary purchases. Remember, with two children we drove a rusted-out 1991 minivan with no air conditioning. Who do I think I am? I still battle these thoughts once in a while. The difference is they don't stick around too long because I can recognize that they are not real or rational. And by the way my parents were really happy for me.

Jasmine's Money Shame Story

"Guilt. Jealousy. Throw on some more Guilt. I grew up with relatives who secretly did not celebrate other people's successes, but who sugar coated what they said with sprinkles and honey. My grandmother and grandfather both believed in hard work. They believed the only way to achieve money is to work until the point of exhaustion. This was how you attained respect. It became a silent competition of who worked the most—some bizarre bragging rights of utter exhaustion and long work days.

"People who had money were gossiped about; they were even considered sinners—'That is not the way of Jesus.' If someone dared to show up at Christmas supper with a new vehicle or something that was expensive that they were proud of, it was met with comments such as 'Oh, it must be nice to have extra money ...' in a sweet, dripping sarcastic tone. It was followed with a 'We certainly never had that kind of extra money when we were your age.'

"My family learned to downplay 'things' we acquired. I would have to justify my new jacket with a pre-emptive 'Mom got it on clearance and that's the only reason she bought it for me; she would never pay full price for anything!' I dare not say how much I loved it. It was more like a 'I'm just so thankful that I am able to wear a jacket.' If going to Grandma's house meant I had to downplay the money my parents worked for in order to feel accepted, that's what I learned to do.

"As I grew up, I learned to act and think like I was struggling and poor—that seemed to earn me respect. When my husband and I bought a new home, I remember being so proud, but I had this sick feeling when I knew my grandparents were coming over. Without even processing or realizing what I was doing, I was acting, looking, and feeling poor in order to feel good around them. I normally would have opened my door proudly to show off my new home, but instead I opened it sheepishly. I quickly explained that it looked as though it cost more than it did, and that it was actually cheaper than buying an older home and fixing it up. This ensured that I fit in with my family.

"Looking back, it is so clear to me why I have been terrified of financial success—it felt bad. It is so clear to me why I have found comfort being in debt—it ensured my place in the family. If I were genuinely worried about money and had to stick to a strict budget, it meant I didn't have to play the role, and could be authentic. I could be a worried, stressed version of myself, and I didn't have to play a role. It meant I was accepted for who I was.

"As the years have gone on and I have recognized this pattern, I have learned to let it go. I deserve to be financially stable and wealthy, and there is no longer any shame attached to that."

Our stories can come from a place of scarcity or from a

place of abundance. Both of these attitudes can be present through our money history and they flow through different cycles of time in our life.

The scarcity loop equals fear, meaning anxiety and stress, creating negative outcomes and poor choices, and feelings of "I don't have enough."

The abundance loop equals gratitude and thankfulness, peace of mind with my money, making wise money decisions with positive outcomes, and feelings of "I have enough."

Arianna's Money Story

"I have roller coaster memories about money from when I was a child. Intense highs and lows. Money was abundant during the early years, and then times became tough in our house, before they got better again. My earliest memories are when Dad changed jobs frequently after the family business ended. Mom watched coupons daily. This was a time when there was a lot of anxiety in our house. It wasn't really talked about, but as a child I could feel it. I felt it when we went grocery shopping; I felt it when it was time for back-to-school shopping. I felt it when my mom had to take a part-time job and leave me with my sister who would always lovingly beat me up. Oh, how I cried, when she had to go to work instead of be at home with me. I hated it.

"I have one vivid childhood memory of driving around on Mother's Day when I was a young girl. I remember being happy and excitedly whining for French fries as we drove past a fast food restaurant. I really, really wanted a treat and French fries were perfect. We never ordered takeout food, ever! It wasn't even an option. So, as I thought about how special it would be to get some French fries, I became relentless, tantruming almost.

"Dad got quiet as we drove past. I was determined and really whining now. Mom said she didn't really want a treat and Dad seemed almost angry. I knew when to stop my tantrum. As we drove on, I remember feeling sad, like I wasn't heard or was being ignored. It hurt my feelings, because I just wanted the day to feel special for Mom. I never asked for stuff like that, and I couldn't understand why there wasn't an exception on this day.

"My dad had to explain to us that we didn't have the money. Not even the five dollars extra that fries would have cost. It just wasn't there. As much as he wanted to stop and buy his family a special something, he just couldn't. Our car became very quiet as I remember processing that. I was scared. For the first time, I felt really, really scared, because money seemed to dictate what we could do, and at that moment money made me feel hopeless and sad. I knew it was one thing not to get new clothes on a regular basis, but there was something that felt very unsettling and unsafe about not being able to afford French fries on a special day.

"Dad carried the shame and guilt of that day for almost a decade. He felt like a failure, and, as scared as I was, I later learned that he was terrified.

"During that time of my childhood, money was tight, very, very tight. There was always food on the table, but bills were barely paid, and there was always the feeling of anxiety over money. Dad went through a depression and Mom took on part-time jobs. Our family was always so close, but I remember these years being hard and scary. Mom was always very spiritual and she always put her trust in God, trusting that we would be okay. She taught me that God answers money prayers too, if they come from a good heart. Dad was a hard worker and full of determination, and he was tired of working for other people, so he did what all brave people who want to earn unlimited earnings do—he started his own business. Dad's business became very successful after a few short years of hard work. Times became good again.

"I had very generous parents who would always give me money—all the time. Just because they could, because they wanted to. When I was old enough to drive, Dad bought me a car. With the car came gas money, which eventually got upgraded to a Visa credit card. This Visa gave my dad peace of mind that I would never be stranded or need to ask for assistance from dangerous strangers. But, I was quite lucky because the most dangerous emergency I ever had to encounter was not having enough money for the cigarette habit I developed as a teen. My Visa took care of that for me, and the receipt just looked like it was part of the fuel bill. I wanted for nothing, and my parents took pride in that.

"By the time I was twenty-two, my parents had paid for my university degree. They never once pushed me to get a job while I studied, because it was so important to them that I use my time for school, and not be distracted by a part-time job.

"My blessed, always-paid-off-Visa-life came to an end shortly after I married in my mid-twenties. My husband had a well-paying job, and I took the big girl step of budgeting his monthly paycheques, while I stayed home to care for our baby. Spending my dad's money was much more fun.

Now I panicked about bills. "What happens if we can't make a mortgage payment?" Living was expensive—groceries, insurance, gas, diapers, another baby on the way.

"Those childhood years of tough times came flooding back with a vengeance! I panicked like it was nobody's business. My husband was thoroughly annoyed. He had his first job at fourteen, bought his first car, and if he didn't have money for gas, he didn't fill it up. WHAT?? No, that didn't make any sense to me. Surely, someone made sure that didn't happen? Nope. According to him, it was only the entitled brats of the world—one of whom he had married—who had those privileges.

"What I was learning about myself during this time was that I had the mentality of a spoiled brat, because that was how the last decade had been for me. I wanted for nothing—even my gel nails were paid for! But deep down I carried the anxiety of my childhood. It just hadn't had a chance to resurface until then.

"All of a sudden, everything always felt so unsafe where money was concerned. My brain filled with a lot of 'what-ifs.' I didn't realize how much my childhood memories were playing a role in that. I had an intense fear that we couldn't afford living. It just seemed normal to worry that money could all go away as fast as it came in. I could never shake this feeling. So I spent. I spent on the house, I spent on the kids. The spending and the amount owing on the Visa almost validated my worry. It justified why I was scared, because after all, look at the bills we had to pay! I NEEDED to feel anxiety about money—that felt normal and comfortable, so I began creating it.

"I was re-creating my childhood fear so that I could justify the fear that I already carried deep in my memory. It seems ridiculous as I write this down, but that state of worry made me feel comfortable. This went on for another decade. There was one particular day when my panic about money reached an unbelievable state. I called my dad crying. Crying! A grown married woman, with two kids, and what most would consider financial security and yet I could not get my anxiety under control. I became a child, and my dad stepped in as the comforting parent. I guess he could see himself in me, in that moment. He dropped what he was doing to make sure I was okay. I secretly think he felt responsible for it, so he did what he could to help me get out of my own brain.

"So, it took me a decade to be okay with the unexpected costs associated with raising a family and paying bills.

"Now, I make my own money to help support my family of four. I've learned how to budget and not panic when money seems tight. But the panic is never far away. It's not even a rational, temporary panic; it's the feeling as-though-my-world-is-slipping-through-my-hands kind of panic that I have to keep in check. I have highs and lows with money.

"I have conflicting childhood memories about money. Feeling rich and feeling poor. So it's easy for my panic to set in during the good times, because I have had to rewire my brain. I have this sense that the wealth can't or won't last. I know this is untrue, but it is very hard to unlearn something.

"I have my mom's strong spirituality and my dad's drive for success. I thank God every day that my husband and I both have secure predictable jobs, because that means security and predictability. But my dad's entrepreneurial spirit is alive in me—however, there's a sense of anxiety that I have to keep at bay when I think about working for myself. I struggle with following my dream of starting a business and collecting a safe paycheque. So for now, I'm doing both. I've found some sort of safety net in that. I've learned that I can create my own money story. I need to take the lessons of scarcity, abundance, and what it means to love, which my family went through, and know that some of those memories still serve me. The other lessons I need to let go."

Memories of the past mixed with the actions of the present somehow entwine and commingle to create our beliefs and behaviours around money today. Remember that by recognizing and honouring the past, we can learn from it and move on.

What is your money story?

Chapter 3—Relationships

"The way you manage money with your partner is a mirror of the ways you handle (or don't) all kinds of issues in your relationship."
Jackie Black, PhD, Board Certified Coach

At some point relationships grow and become more serious. This is when questions start to arise about long-term plans and money. However, the topic is about more than building wealth. It is a deeper conversation that shares beliefs and values about spending and saving.

My husband and I skipped these discussions early in our relationship. We met when I was twenty-one and married soon after. Being a broke student at the time, I believe that our first money conversation and fight was around throwing out pop cans instead of recycling them for pizza money.

It took almost a decade for me to realize how important money is in a relationship. My career was beginning in finance and my life was becoming the place to practice my passion. I have learned things along the way from books, courses, and gaining my professional designations, but more importantly from practice. And while I can't claim that my husband and I are perfect when it comes to money and relationships, I can say that we have come a long way. We have shared our money journeys and we have come to understand and honour each other's money mindsets. We worked hard and our goals and values have aligned.

One of the biggest causes of dispute in relationships is the lack of communication around your differences in values, goals, and habits when it comes to money. Everyone has a unique money history, story, and belief set that can overshadow partnerships and cause disagreements.

One couple I met with were not agreeing about their money during one of our financial planning meetings. He wanted them to take on more debt and renovate their kitchen and buy a brand new car in the near future. She was adamant that they not spend a dime and just continue to save and stash away as much as they could. The discussion was getting heated and obviously had caused fights lately.

I asked each of them to take a timeout from our conversation and share a story with me. I asked each of them to reflect on their first money memory, the first time they could remember the concept of money. She shared that her memory was of wearing a hand-me-down dress from Sears Bargain Center and feeling embarrassed in front of her classmates. She felt as though there was never enough and that her family never had money. Her memory came from a place of scarcity and a fear of not enough. Her husband shared that he took coins from his parents' dresser. His parents never said anything or stopped him; he would take the change down to the store and buy candy or gum each time. He knew that the coins would buy him something whenever he wanted. He came from a place of abundance because there was a plentiful supply of money and always enough to buy what was desired.

It was then with tears in their eyes that they understood each other's money memory and why each of them had a different belief. Each understood where the other was coming from. She was coming from a place of scarcity and fear, and he was coming from a place of abundance and always having enough with no fear of risk or debt. Because of the connections they each made with their own beliefs from the past, they could honour and respect each other's feelings and come to a compromise.

They took each other's hands and asked what they should do. We made a short-term strategy that included enacting a two-year savings plan before they made any purchases and prioritizing the new car over a kitchen renovation once their savings had accumulated.

Avoiding the Money Bombs

I like to think that as couples get to know each other, they start to share their history, dreams, hopes, and aspirations. It is as a relationship starts to get more serious that the money talks need to happen. This might be in bite-size small steps in the early stages, but should progress to include full transparency.

Full Disclosure in Your Relationship

This is what I know. Ensure there is full disclosure in your relationship.

I remember not telling my husband that I had an unpaid Sears credit card bill, because I was embarrassed about having an amount owing. To my surprise, I was even more embarrassed when we applied for our first mortgage back in 1996 and the banker asked my husband about that outstanding bill. He had no idea and it caused more stress than if I had shared my circumstance.

Finding the Right Time

There is never the *right* time to talk about money. You just schedule it, make a date, and make it happen.

Most of us talk about money when we are deciding to buy something or when the bills come in. Such conversations can cause stress, because they force us to talk about money. Situational conversation is stressful because of the surrounding circumstances. Such money talks happening out of necessity do not come from a positive place. They occur when there is a feeling of scarcity or a lack of money. This is often when the "money bombs" start to fall. They might sound like this, "You spent how much! How could you have done that! Why did you buy that? We can't afford it." Money bombs hurt. By scheduling a regular time to talk, these bombs can be defused.

Make separate lists of the things you want to cover. Think of every money question and concern you can think of. Share your goals and work to determine what is important to each of you with a vision of where you both want to be in five years.

I like to schedule this time for talking about money when we don't have other family distractions. After work or at bedtime is generally not a great time because we can feel rushed or exhausted. In our house, Saturday or Sunday mornings when we are alone and having our coffee work best for financial check-ins. After a money talk and check-in, try a walk around the park. It will bring a sense of peace, abundance, and gratitude.

Communicating

I can't remember from early on in my marriage if one of us handled the finances more than the other. I feel as though we had so little that there wasn't much to plan or talk about, it just all got spent (sometimes, a few days before the next payday). We were blessed to have family that supported us emotionally, and financially as well at times. We borrowed money from my husband's parents for the down payment on our first house. In 1996, we borrowed $2,500 for our $40,000 home. We then had to renovate it once the front roof caved in during a heavy snow fall, but even then our parents helped with labour, love, and at times money.

We were so blessed to have the emotional support of our parents. I think that must have alleviated most of the financial stress. Our families made us feel secure and guided us through a lot of growing up and adult responsibilities that come with learning to be parents ourselves and purchasing a house. My husband and I functioned as a team at that time, communicating and collaborating. I know it wasn't all rainbow and unicorns. I do have many memories of hard times and having to leave groceries at the till because we didn't have enough money, but it was temporary stress that—due to our naivety and blissful ignorance—felt like it passed quickly until the next payday.

It was as we got older that things became more complicated. I remember being told that the more money we made, the more we would spend. Even as I stayed home to raise our daughters, my husband's income continued to increase but there wasn't magically more money. Life became more expensive. We managed and accepted the sacrifices so that I could stay home until my younger daughter started school full time. Somewhere in all of this, our communication died and our relationship became strained. By default I became the person who took care of everything from children, pets, activities, and house, to paying the bills. Those were the dark days leading up to my marriage breakdown. The stress must have taken a toll on me because somewhere in the mix of it all, the water was turned off. I had forgotten to pay a bill and must have ignored a warning letter. We had the money. Money was not the problem. The problem was the burden of having to manage it all. We were no longer collaborating or communicating. So even if money is not the problem, it can become the symptom that appears out of something bigger.

Supporting and Collaborating

Money problems are one of the leading factors of marriage breakdowns. I believe it is vital for both parties in a relationship to be aware of their financial situation and be a part of the financial decision-making. I am not necessarily talking about the day-to-day transactions, because generally there is one person over another who manages the simple bill paying. Bill paying is different than shouldering all of the financial responsibility and big-picture planning. Allowing one person the sole responsibility of keeping an eye on the family money and future can cause hidden anxiety and stress for both partners.

Mark, a friend and small business owner, recently severed ties with his old business partner. The acrimonious dissolution of their long association left Mark bitter and financially strained. Before the partnership ended, Mark and his wife, who had a successful career, had celebrated the birth of their first child and purchased a larger home. Their future was bright.

Two years later, the continuing accumulation of legal, real estate, and accounting fees combined with everyday living expenses took a tremendous toll on Mark's well-being. When I talked with him, I learned that he had been hospitalized with a stress-induced illness, which he thought at the time was a heart attack.

Mark confided in me that he felt forced to borrow money from his family, unbeknownst to his wife, because he did not want to share with her the stress he incurred. Mark has been carrying the burden of his family finances and is a walking time bomb. He is only thirty-two years old!

Your Biggest Wealth

The health of your mind, body, and relationships is your biggest wealth.

It is fair to want and need support and collaboration to run a household and manage the family finances. One person may want to do all of this alone, but creating a team approach is the best.

In our house, I am the organizer of our day-to-day finances. I am a financial planner and manage millions of dollars successfully, but even an expert needs support and collaboration at home from family members. My husband and I sit down together on a scheduled basis and make sure that we are on the same page. We discuss any purchases coming up that will need paying. We have tried to unify our money conversations and include our two teens. Having my husband just sit next to me while I review the bank accounts and organize our cash flow makes me feel supported. Don't get me wrong, I like the responsibility of organizing our cash flow. I want control of our daily finances. It gives me peace of mind and confidence and it gets done.

In most of the families I work with, it is the woman who has led the need for structure and control. She can do it all and may want to do it all but, like me, she would probably enjoy feeling supported. For myself, it feels caring when my husband has a coffee and sits with me while I pay the bills and complete our monthly banking. Some of our best money conversations have happened during these times.

Your partner doesn't have to literally pay the bills with you but his being present, sitting next to you, and listening to you, allows for the two of you to be able to communicate your needs in that moment.

Do you need reassurance to move away from the scarcity mindset edge, or do you want to share how well you are doing and high five each other for making it through another month in the black? Key are the conversations and emotions that come out when being physically present with each other.

Sex and Money

It's hard to not open a magazine or article that has the title: "How to keep love alive." You will read tips on ways to keep the spark going, how to be there for your partner, and how to weather the storms. But not one of those articles shares that to keep the romance and sex alive all you have to do is sit next to me while I pay the bills and review our bank accounts.

When I feel the most connected with and supported by my partner, there is plenty of sex. We make time for one another. In our finances, an abundance mindset is the belief that there will be enough, there is opportunity, hope, and gratitude. The benefits of adopting and constantly choosing this mindset are that it flows into all other aspects of our life, including the bedroom.

Researchers at Dartmouth College, US, and the University of Warwick, England, measured levels of happiness in sixteen thousand men and women. They found that the more sex people had, the happier they were, regardless of their age or whether they were male or female.[6]

The researchers also found that sex is so closely tied to happiness that they estimated increasing sexual intercourse from once a month to once a week would have the same mood-boosting effects as adding $50,000 a year in income.

Would You Rather Talk about Sex or Money?

I asked my husband whether he would rather talk about sex than money and he chose sex in a record speed-of-light response. I then asked him if he thinks about money more than sex (because I am pretty sure that I do). Just as quickly he replied, "No way"; he thinks way more about sex.

So does that make me the only one out there? Is this a gender thing? I had to surf the web to put my mind at ease. A Harris Poll reveals that three in four American women think more about money than sex and that worrying about it lowers their sexual desire.[7]

A scarcity mindset can cause money problems that then show up in the bedroom and this can wreak havoc under the sheets without even realizing it. Financial fear, worry, and lack of confidence are scarcity barriers that women struggle with. Having money talks outside the bedroom help as does checking the scarcity mindset at the door before climbing into bed. An abundance mindset means more sex.

Financially Compatible

> I asked Carly, has money ever crept into the bedroom for her? Is there a correlation between an abundant versus scarcity mindset and romance?
>
> "From a salary perspective, I've earned six figures for many years. To be blunt, I want to date someone who makes close to equivalent or more than me. Not being on a similar playing field income wise, I always would be a rub ... particularly to the male ego!"

Lesson Learned

I've met with women who have come to me after the death of their partner and had no idea what their financial circumstance was or what their partner's last wishes were.

I have met surviving spouses who had no idea that their partner had gambled away all of their savings, who had no idea where the statement of accounts and investments was located, and who did not know if there was life insurance or a will.

My grandparents passed away at the age of ninety-two, within a few months of each other. What a love story. During my lifetime, they taught me many lessons and left me great memories. I believe that my grandparents did not realize their last lesson and gift to my family would be the importance of sharing their information and communicating their wishes.

My mother had retired before my grandparents needed care. She had the time and ability to be their caregiver. This was a blessing, but not a common one. Due to work and other family obligations, it is not often that a family member can become a caregiver. Grandpa and my mother became close. During that time, he shared with her where he stored all the estate planning needs. He had everything in order—all his bills, his account statements, his funeral wishes, even the invitation list. Grandpa was as sharp as a tack and more organized than Martha Stewart. He kept a Tupperware file alphabetized with documents, wills, and funeral plans.

My parents are young and in their sixties, but because of the example left by my grandparents, we have had the same conversations and I have adopted the same practice with my own clients. I give my clients a binder as a way to organize all their important life documents to prepare for the what ifs in their lives so that their families have access and answers. The binder is for gathering a list of important contacts, account and asset information, business interests, and other financial information. Also, there is a section called, "If Something Happens to Me." This is where they can document their wishes and intentions.

Vulnerability

My mom grew up a young woman in the Gloria Steinem era, marching and protesting in the 1960s and 1970s for women's rights. She was one of the first permanent female employees to be hired as a labourer in the roadways department for the City of Regina. Her career was in a man's world her entire working life. The year she retired at age sixty, she was still wearing steel toe boots and filling potholes in our city streets. I grew up proud of her and very aware of the gender difference and disparity that she worked against during her career. I also grew up knowing the importance of a woman's independence—the ability to stand on her own two feet on her own terms.

As a very young child I was witness to my single mom's struggle in the early years. And even recognizing all of this, I left myself vulnerable ten years ago. I was embarrassed, and still am to this day, that I had put myself in a position that was against everything my parents had taught me and wanted for me—I lost my financial identity. It was as though I no longer existed. I did not have any credit in my name, I had no bank account in my name, and everything was financially connected to the identity of my husband. I had no full-time employment, no income on my income tax return. In fact, I was labelled a dependent according to Canada Revenue Agency. I learned the hard way how vital it is for each spouse to maintain a separate credit card, regardless of who makes the money.

I could have handled being a dependent if I knew that I had protected myself along the way financially. But I hadn't.

I remember trying to change the utilities into my name after my husband moved out. I couldn't even get the home telephone in my name. I had to call my husband and get his approval to co-sign the phone in my name. I had left myself vulnerable. I made the mistake of not having my own individual credit cards. Even a credit limit of $500 would have sufficed and shown up favourably on a credit score. University students can receive a thousand dollars credit without employment.

The consequence of having all our credit joint with my husband as the primary owner was devastating. Taking care of our own financial identity is not about planning for the demise of our relationships. Instead, it promotes a sense of well-being, self-love, self-care, independence, and confidence. These emotions work to enhance our partnership and our love.

After my husband and I had separated and I started working full time, I set out to build my own credit rating. I had saved enough money to buy a piece of furniture from Pier One and I knew that if I applied for the Pier One credit card, I would receive an additional 20 percent off my first purchase. I applied for my first credit card that day in the Pier One store. I can remember that moment so clearly. I stood in total fear waiting as she called the credit agency to accept my application. I was so panicked and worried. My fingers were crossed as I stood there. Eventually I was approved. Afterwards, I cried in the car with tears of relief and joy, but they were also mixed with shame of being thirty-something years old and having no financial identity. I paid the balance off immediately and I have not used the credit card since, but it is in my purse and I will not part with it. I look at it to remind myself often of the significance of that day for me.

Here is what I learned:

1. Have a credit card solely in your own name.
2. Have your own savings account. This is not hidden money or a squirrel cash stash that promotes secrecy. Rather it is a bank account in your own name with some money in it that you can access in an emergency.
3. Keep your credit history healthy and maintain a good credit score. You can check your credit reports at wwwtransunion.ca and at www.consumer.equifax.ca.
4. Each spouse or partner will need to complete a will. Along with your will, you should each have a power of attorney and a health directive. I also suggest you talk with each other to share your wishes if something were to happen to you.

Linda's Money Story

"As a divorced and remarried baby boomer mother and grandmother, I have many recollections of money, especially relating to empowerment.

"I was the youngest of three children raised on a small mixed farm in Saskatchewan. Our home was modest, to say the least. We had no running water or indoor toilet. My mother cooked on a wood-burning stove on which she heated water for laundry and baths. (My grandchildren are amazed that people actually lived this way.) So, yes, we were poor, but we were provided for with life's necessities and we did not know any differently.

"My first 'have not' memory is having to ride a used bicycle, while my older siblings had received new bikes at a younger age. My parents always felt guilty for not having the money for this purchase, and at the age of twenty-two, when I had a child of my own, my dad bought me a brand new bike! They also could not afford to pay for my sister's and my weddings, so we paid for them ourselves and thought nothing of it. But we also planned simple, cost-effective weddings, certainly not the extravagant celebrations of the day.

"My husband grew up with similar values in a family of five, and consequently we taught our three children to work for what they wanted. In hindsight was this the best strategy? I don't know. Do their first money memories consist of delivering flyers at age ten or working at a restaurant to fund a school trip to New York? Whether they were taught about money in a responsible or fear-based manner, they all put themselves through post-secondary education and they have successful careers.

"Divorce presents a whole new dimension to thoughts about money—not fear so much as the necessity of making decisions on one's own, knowing that, right or wrong, there is no one to rely on or to blame.

"When I divorced and soon after lost my job, I established a relationship with a financial advisor and have never looked back. Oh, I still made, and I continue to make, some impetuous, fearless decisions, but I have few regrets.

> "Life is meant to be lived and enjoyed. My dad used to say, 'Money makes the world go round.'"

By talking openly about money and emotions, you can make your relationship stronger and more connected. Along the way you might also just become more financially savvy.

What is your experience with money within your relationship?

Do you have a system or process in place to avoid the money bombs?

Chapter 4—Children and Money

"Happiness is when what you think, what you say, and what you do are in harmony."
Mahatma Gandhi[8]

Stanford University conducted an interesting experiment in the late 1960s.[9] The university studied hundreds of children, who were mostly at the ages of four and five, and the idea of instant gratification. Each child was sat in a chair in a room alone and given a marshmallow. They were each told that the researcher had to leave the room, and that they would be rewarded with a second marshmallow if the child did not eat the one in front of them. If they could sit and wait, they could then have two marshmallows. If they ate the one marshmallow right away, they would not receive another one. The idea was that if the child could practise self-control, they would be rewarded.

The researcher would leave for fifteen minutes and then return. There are similar current-day recreations of this experiment on YouTube and the video footage is entertaining. You can just imagine the temptation. Children are licking the marshmallow obsessively, pinching off small pieces, sitting on their hands, jumping, and wiggling, while some just pop it in their mouth instantly.

The original experiment at Stanford continued up to forty years later with the same children. The researchers followed up and tracked each child and found a positive correlation between delaying instant gratification and success later in life. Different areas in life were measured—SAT scores, substance abuse, obesity, stress, and social skills.

I know that there are many more compounding factors than delaying instant gratification that dictate whether or not a person will be successful in all areas of life. But this experiment became popular because it is an easy way for us to recognize that discipline and delaying instant gratification are habits that should not be ignored. We can train our conscious mind to become aware of the difference between our present self and our future self, and choose to delay something so our future self can benefit.

I am going to be honest. I am awful at being patient. I complain and moan and possibly obsess if I have to delay or wait for something that is important to me. I probably would have been a child in the marshmallow test who gulped the treat down in seconds. However, over time, I have learned to recognize my impatience and with practice I have learned the benefits of delaying instant gratification. The only way to install and promote this habit is to practise it ourselves. This is the same strategy that I try with my children—practise the habit of waiting. It is a hard thing to teach, because it is not just one lesson, but rather a lesson over a lifetime. The sooner we can recognize the opportunities to teach delaying instant gratification, the easier the lessons become.

By the way, delayed gratification does not mean no gratification.

I remember many outbursts because my young children wanted dessert before supper, or they wanted the treat at the grocery store. In the moment, the easy thing to do as a parent is to give in and make all the loud, nagging tantrums go away. But, by delaying the urge to make the unpleasantness go away, I am preparing myself and my children to habituate delayed gratification and patience.

Here is what I learned from the marshmallow test:

When the researchers covered the marshmallows, the children were less tempted. This leads me to believe that out of sight, out of mind might be an effective strategy to help children from being overwhelmed. In fact, I think this strategy probably works with me too. If I can stay out of a shoe store or a shopping centre, I have no desire to purchase shoes. With our children, removing temptation is a great habit. The treats and cookies generally go in a cupboard, but the fruit and veggies can be pre-cut in plain sight in the fridge ready to go. The same thing can be done with computers and screen time by putting iPads and phones away to keep screen time down. When my children were much younger and I stayed home with them, we had bought an armoire for our television so that it was behind closed doors. The cupboard doors would stay shut until it was the planned time to watch television. This helped in limiting their desire to watch during the day.

When the researchers told the children to think happy thoughts, some of the children would sing songs or talk to themselves. By distracting themselves, the children were able to wait successfully without eating the marshmallow.

In fact, the children who were given a slinky to play with were almost all successful in waiting. By keeping busy and changing their focus to a positive distraction, we can teach our children to delay immediate gratification. This is again about habit and building a routine that can stick for years to come.

Researchers found that some of the children would talk to themselves with affirmative statements like, "I can wait, I can wait. If I wait, I can have more." These affirmations become almost a mantra that the children taught themselves. Teaching phrases that are easy to repeat can be very helpful and also very easy.

Money Stories Parents Taught

I asked women whom I know, some with families of their own and some without, to share what they remember their parents teaching them about money. I asked them what money messages they received growing up. Parents teach us a lot of lessons in life, some on purpose and some by accident. I don't think there is any greater influence on children than from their family. We have learned what to do and what not to do from watching and listening to our parents. We each have a unique upbringing different from anyone else's and because of that I am always curious to hear about how unique stories and pasts can convert into money messages.

Hard Work and Independence, Julie's Story

"I never grew up thinking we didn't have money but looking

back I am sure things were tight. For example, when we went out for supper we were told that we could only have water, and we couldn't order a drink. In a family of four kids, things like that add up. We always took part in activities though, and I never wished for more or felt we didn't have enough.

"As we got older we were given an allowance. We learned the value of not only money, but of working for what we wanted. I remember going to the credit union and opening my first account, being taught how to record transactions, and keeping a balance.

"As I got older, I remember my grandparents always saying that if you couldn't pay by cash you shouldn't buy it. I know I put off getting a credit card for a long time thinking about this, and when I finally did get one, I tried to use it only for larger purchases. Even though that isn't always the case, I make sure that I am always paying it off. My grandparents' views on money and purchases have stuck with me.

"As I prepared for university, I worked hard in two and three jobs at a time. I came from a family that worked hard. I believe that hard work and sound finances, in many regards, go hand in hand. I went through seven years of university only having my first year paid for me. I never took out a single loan. Doing this, I valued the fact that I did it on my own, which means so much. I valued the hard work and appreciated that it was not just handed to me.

"To this day, I continue to try and do things on my own. In purchasing my first home, I didn't want anyone else to have to be financially responsible for it.

"Times are often tight, which results in me being more aware of what I have and what I am spending it on. My parents talk more now about what they thought we didn't have and the sacrifices that were made, more than I was ever aware of; but I think we just aren't aware when we are young. I notice how money affects so many today and so much is just handed to youth. They have no concept of what it means to save or work for something.

"I am thankful I learned about finances. Even as an adult I am learning more about what I need to do to prepare for my future—something that I believe is important and needs to be started early in life."

Lake Toys—Saving for the Inflatable Tubes and Boats, Carly's Story

"My siblings and I sold eggs in town to raise money for our lake toys. It took a lot of a-dollar-a-dozen sales to buy something substantial with our 'egg money.' We would also each raise a calf from spring until fall and it would be sold for our RESPs. Being involved in branding, etc. was part of that work. I think the lessons my parents taught me were to be frugal when you can, but buy quality when you do, and you need to work for your money. And ... save, save, save."

Carly's Lesson of Consequence

"I remember it had been a terrible weather year on the farm. And when your income is entirely dependent on that, there can be some lean years—no income for a whole year! My high school was going on a ski trip that year and it shocked me that I might not be able to go because money was so tight."

Anna's Lesson of Value and Appreciation

> "I think one of the biggest lessons I learned is to value what we work for. Stuff was not just handed to us. We were definitely helped out, we had a car to share among three of us as we went to university, and we lived at home for free. But we also had to have a job and save in order to pay for university. I appreciate what I had, what I bought, and what I earned."

Harmony

I feel as though I have started late in life with attempting to share a healthy relationship with money with my daughters. I never truly began my own journey to my money story until my marriage was ending. In the early years (okay, including the present moment as well), I have made parenting mistakes that I wish I could reverse. I would like a few do-overs.

I often reminisce back to when my daughters were young. Maybe I shouldn't have let them cry it out as one-year-olds. What if I had nursed them longer, would they have no allergies today? "I should have, I could have" plays out in every woman's head. All the love in the world isn't going to shelter us from making mistakes. The challenge that comes from this is being able to embrace our humanity and not punish ourselves. We all need self-compassion and self-love.

The same is true with our relationship with money because how you feel about yourself will affect how you handle money. Also, how you handle money will affect your children. This is a cycle that can become positive. By creating a thriving, abundant, healthy attitude with your own money, you can then pass on that same healthy attitude to your children. Like a sponge, they will soak up the attitudes and beliefs around them, even when you think they are too young to understand.

Teaching our children about money is more than a conversation. It is making a commitment to recognizing our own personal money stories. As a parent, we can define what money means to each of us and then decide what values and beliefs we want our children to grow up with. However, our words and wants need to align with our actions. When they don't match, our children will notice.

My older daughter Mikayla and I were recently out for a walk around the park with our dog. We were chatting and enjoying the beautiful sunset and summer weather. I had mentioned that it would be nice to plan another family vacation to Tofino and rent a house on the beach. We had done that a few years back and it was one of my favourite places to be with family and friends. My daughter responded, "Yes, that would be great. But this time can you not stress about money the whole time? I felt stressed about it."

I stopped abruptly in the middle of the walking path with our dog, causing the couple behind us to have to swerve to the side to go around us to avoid a pile up. I was shocked. We had saved and planned for that trip and had plenty of money. My initial reaction was very defensive. I thought I did everything I was supposed to as leader of my tribe—we had the cash flow plan, we knew our family priorities and values, we communicated, and I thought we felt free and unconstrained because of our positive abundant harmony.

What did I miss?

I think the answer is I tried too hard. My daughter shared with me that she would hear a few conversations in the kitchen of me and my husband checking in with the prices of the surf lessons or the price of the groceries. It was routine conversation to me and part of my cash flow process, but those discussions projected worry on to my daughter.

I was not in harmony with our true family value of "freedom." I was so attached to our cash flow plan that I did not recognize when to release it when needed so that we could feel our purpose of freedom. Vacations are supposed to be a way to feel our family's freedom and give us a break from our duties so that we can forget them and just enjoy family and friends. I have learned that I need to release our systems at times and take breaks to enjoy life. I wouldn't have learned this lesson had my daughter not felt open enough to communicate with me how she felt. So, not only did I learn to release and let go when needed, but I also confirmed the importance of having open communication and checking in. I let my daughter know that I wasn't perfect, but that I am human and I will try to grow from this.

Money Messages

What message do I think I am sending to my children about money? What do I want my child to learn?

I hope that my daughters feel safe and happy and

abundant. I want them to feel empowered over their money choices with a positive healthy attitude.

I asked my younger daughter Izzy, who is in her last year of high school, to share with me what money message she has picked up.

"To be frugal with conscious spending. It is okay to spend money and splurge as long as it is planned and you have prepared for it," she replied.

I asked her what her first memory was that had to do with the concept of money. She told me that she would have been four or five years old when she had found a loonie in our minivan and had not wanted to keep it. She remembers her dad turning around and telling her that it is not "just" a loonie—a one-dollar coin—but that to some people a dollar would be the start of something that can add up to more.

Her memory seems very fitting for her. She is a saver who is very proud of earning her own money and very proud to spend her own money when she feels it is important. She uses her own earned savings to donate to charity. She also shared the same word that our family values, "freedom."

Send the Right Message

As parents we aren't perfect, no matter how hard we try. We want to install healthy habits and to lead by example, but sometimes it is easy to skip the positive money message because of our own negative thoughts and beliefs. As you work on rewriting your own money beliefs, you can use these tips as reminders to come back to as needed:

- Get your own finances in order so that you can show

your children by example that you are thinking of the future and making conscientious decisions for the family. Be a financial leader.

- Teach early. Our children are never too young to learn healthy habits. Even toddlers can pick up on our attitudes and actions.
- Communicate in a positive manner about money. For example, if bills come in the mail, it is easy to throw a few choice, negative words around and make a comment about not having enough money to pay all the bills. You might be venting, but a child might think you literally mean you have no money. Worry and fear could become associated with common bills.

Jennifer's Story

"My girls have been given an 'allowance' since they were four years old. It's one dollar per year of age and I pay it at the end of the month. I try to stress that the allowance is because we all work together as a team to keep our house clean and running smoothly and not for the chores they do or don't do; it's a thank you for helping out.

"We also use the jar system for their money and they decide what amount goes where.

"My nine-year-old has only two jars: Savings (to go to the bank) and Spending.

"The majority of her money is in her Savings jar because she's a super saver and only likes to spend money on buying gifts for others.

"My thirteen-year-old has three jars: Savings (to go to the bank), Spending, and Phone Savings (she wants a phone for high school). She splits hers evenly between her jars but is very torn and is always looking to do odd jobs for the family in exchange for money.

"They use their spending money when we go on vacation or camping. They decide how much to bring so they can buy 'treats' or items for themselves, such as candy, a T-shirt, etc. (Of course, mom buys the ice cream!) Planning like this makes them think twice and to shop around prior to spending their money because once it's gone, it's gone."

The Jar System

The jar system is not new and I can't remember where I originally read this idea, but it works really well. This is a practice that can be started at age five and all the way through until the end of middle school.

Once children get older, the habit of having these savings jars will extend to the digital world of money. It will make the transition to our online world of banking and plastic cards much easier. Here's how it works:

1. Label Four Jars

   A child uses four jars, labeled with their name and the words "Spend, Save, Give, Invest."

   Spend jar—money they can spend however they choose, as needed.

   Save jar—money they are saving to buy a specific item.

   Give jar—money they will give to a charity of their choice.

   Invest jar—money they will invest to learn about

compound savings with interest over the long-term.

2. Give an Allowance
   Once a week, children can receive an allowance. For young children, it is important to have tangible money in their hands to help them understand. When they receive the allowance, it is equally divided into the jars. Quarters are great coins to start with for five-year-olds. The amount will increase with their age. Parents have shared with me that they like to use a dollar a week per age of their child. That way they have a system to increase each birthday.
3. Use the Spend Jar
   The amount in this jar is intended to be used on a special trip to the store. Whatever amount is in the spend jar can be used to buy an item. This is a great time to communicate the dollar value of an item and whether or not there is enough money in the spend jar. There is usually plenty of opportunity to use a delayed gratification approach because often there is not enough money for the most desired item. This is when a good "save jar" goal is set.
4. Make Choices
   If your child chooses to spend all of the money on a small item, the choice is up to them. However, this is a great time to discuss that if they wait, they can have the item they really want. The key here is to allow freedom and choice. I know it's hard to take, but we need our children to make a few bad purchases so that we can talk about them and hopefully have a learning lesson.

5. Be an Example
   By taking care of your own "jars" and making sure you have organized your finances, you can easily share that planning with your children and communicate how you spend your own money.

How to Teach Young Children about Money

At Age Five

Here are some terms that can be explained in the right situation:

- **Goal**—working toward saving for something means knowing its cost and when you want to buy it.
- **Bank**—a safe place that stores our money.
- **Bills**—notices letting us know what we haven't paid for yet, like electricity and what we still owe for purchases.
- **Book**—The Berenstain Bears' Dollars and Sense, by Stan Berenstain and Jan Berenstain, in which Mama gives her cubs an allowance and guides them through the consequences of impulse spending.

At Age Ten

- **Interest**—money that is added to money you either borrow or save.
- **Loan**—borrowed money that must be repaid.
- **Inflation**—the increase each year on the cost of things.

- **Taxes**—money that we pay the government to help pay for public programs and essentials.
- **Credit cards and debit cards**—the differences between the two.
- **Game**—Monopoly has many teachable moments and includes risks versus rewards.

At Age Fifteen

- **Assets**—valuables or resources that have a monetary value
- **Investing**—using assets to help your money grow over time.
- **Diversification**—spreading money across various savings methods.
- **Stock**—a share of a public company.
- **Compounding interest**—interest that is added to an original amount and then accumulates with interest on the interest. For example, if you were to save $50 per month with 7 percent interest from age fifteen until age fifty-five, you would accumulate $124,000.By this age children are ready for a bank account for students that has no fees. The jar system template should still be maintained but now be completed using bank accounts.

Tasking

I remember the first time my daughters took our shopping list and bought the groceries themselves. Mikayla was in grade eight and Izzy in grade six. I dropped them off at the front door of the grocery store.

I wish I could tell you that I had planned the experience to be a teaching moment and a lesson for my daughters in shopping. But, honestly, I was exhausted and tired and the last thing I wanted to do was go in the store. I dropped them off and went to get myself a latte and wait for them.

I will never forget that first-time shopping experience, not because of the great life lesson opportunities, but only for the fact that I became a super hero legend in our neighborhood. On that Saturday, my daughters ran into families from our street. Apparently, each of the parents asked what aisle I was in because they wanted to say hello and chat. When my daughters told them I wasn't at the store, our neighbours' jaws dropped with surprised expressions.

I can't tell you if my daughters stuck close to our cash flow plan, or what amount they spent, or what great financial lessons they learned. The only thing I know is that after that, I made my daughters get groceries often while I went for coffee.

$450!

The supper table conversation in my home recently was used as an update for the last two weeks when I was away for business. The usual conversation entailed who did what and anything new and exciting. When the meal was almost finished, my daughter blurted out, "OMG, I forgot to tell you—groceries for just one week were $450!" I had to bite my tongue, take a deep breath, and comment, "Tell me about your grocery trip."

She continued to describe what she bought and then asked me why it costs so much and if food has always been that expensive. Usually our weekly shopping bill would be under $300. My daughters' shopping trip had included a few extras and a few treats that we usually do not buy. The large bag of bulk pistachios didn't help!

My reply to her question was that no, it had not always cost that much for groceries. I was delighted, even if she was not, to explain to her about inflation. I explained the concept of inflation as being the increase each year in the cost of food and services. So, we are not losing our minds when we walk out of the store carrying only two bags of groceries costing over a hundred dollars and wondering if the cashier made a mistake. I have been known to sit in the car and read the receipt in disbelief, because I was honestly just running in to pick up a few things, not to spend a small fortune.

Because of my profession, I am very aware of the annual statistics. When we are cash flow planning and retirement planning, we need to acknowledge this inflation rate and account for it every year going forward. My family understands why I am aware of the rising cost of goods. It is easy to overspend and not think of the worth of our future dollar. I am full of gratitude and thanks that we eat very well and that we can afford our purchases even with inflation, but I will never pass up a good sale and I do not mind using coupons. So, I think my daughter has a better understanding when I kindly suggest a better (what I actually mean is "cheaper") snack alternative to bulk pistachios!

Mik's First Car

"If you can eat it, drink it, or wear it, it is NOT an emergency to spend your money on!"

That was my comment to my teenage daughter who had accumulated enough savings that they started burning a hole in her pocket. Like every parent, I am trying to teach my two teenage daughters to spend money wisely, save, and survive in our economic world. Easier said than done!

As my older daughter's savings have added up, so has her desire to spend them. After some heated negotiations, she has agreed to use most of her savings to purchase and fix her first car. The car is old and has almost 300,000 kilometres on the clock. She has heard me discuss how many kilometres are on the car and I am sure she could sense the concern in my voice. Her savings paid for the insurance, a new windshield, new brakes, and a new clutch. You can appreciate that with her budget of $2,000, the car is not the one of her dreams.

As parents, we can only hope that we have helped our children do the right thing. We try to lay a foundation that will last a lifetime. I am plagued by doubts at times. Is the car a lemon? Will she actually learn anything from this experience? Am I doing the right thing? The benefit of our teachings can take years to sink in.

As I wait to bear witness to the outcome of my doubts, I have a glimmer of hope that my daughter has benefitted and learned some lessons from spending her own money and taking accountability for a vehicle. Her father and I have been informed, "STOP DRIVING MY CAR! YOU ARE GOING TO USE UP ALL THE KILOMETRES!"

She has heard us talking and debating about the mileage on the car being really high, but in all our efforts, we never explained to her that there was not an expiry of kilometres at a specific amount. I think our next lesson will need to be basic car mechanics!

Best Money Advice

I asked some of my clients, "What was the best money advice you were ever given?" Here are some of the answers.

"Life is not a dress rehearsal: don't finish with any regrets."

"Live below your means. So many people live above their means and, therefore, they don't have money to pay themselves first. If you can live below your means, it will help you immensely in the long run."

"Start a just-in-case fund. You don't want to be stuck in a desperate situation. Financial independence may be able to help you get out of a curveball that life will throw you."

"Don't invest in what you don't understand."

"If you are not careful, the more you make, the more you'll spend."

"The best financial advice I received was to just start saving and investing. Many people will talk about starting and come up with excuses like, 'If I just make a little more money' or 'When I get the next promotion.' The truth is you just need to cut the excuses and start, no matter the amount."

Personal life experiences lead to a mixture of trial and error and learning from the advice of others. One of the advantages of learning from others is that you get the chance to avoid the errors and jump straight to the wins. So, review and ask yourself, "What is the best money advice you have received?"

Chapter 5—Cash Flow

"Our money should have a plan and a purpose and match our heart values."
Zena Amundsen

Talking about money causes a lot of people to automatically tune out with deaf ears and glazed eyes. Some people would rather go to the dentist for a root canal than review their money plan.

When I ask my clients, "What is the most common thought that pops into your head about a money plan?" the answers I receive are "budget; that means boring; it feels like it doesn't work; too time consuming; hard to keep up with; not empowering; restrictive." The list goes on.

Years ago during a financial planning meeting, I would have asked a client, "So how is the family budget? Are you on a budget?"

Away from the office and at home, one might have heard me say, "We need a budget, we are spending way too much this month." It sounds similar to when I go out to eat too many evenings in a row and my pants are tight. I moan, "I need to go on a diet, I am eating way too much."

The word "budget" means the same to me as the word "diet." And "diet" to me means scarcity, slim pickings, and not enough.

For example, if a budget plan restricts my latte purchases and I am told that I can no longer buy my Grand Non-Fat Chai Latte with a Shot of Espresso every other day, you would have to physically drag me away and restrain me from entering Starbucks. Some financial books label this the "latte factor." The latte factor is a money-saving strategy that recommends redirecting your money from small things (like daily lattes) to savings to increase your wealth. I cannot and I will not give up my latte. It might work temporarily but I will not be able to sustain this as a long-term strategy. I can foresee that my failure at maintaining the latte savings would then have me feeling like a failure, letting my family down, and just ending up with me magnifying the scarcity loop. I would rather give up buying my expensive department store facial cream and name brand toilet paper than my coffee! (And by the way I have and it's so worth it for my latte!)

Aligning Your Own Personal Values

Rather than using the term "budget," I like to use the term "cash flow." Your cash flow is the amount of money that is moving in and out of your household. It means you have the power to control the flow.

I decided to train with Stephanie Holmes-Winton, author, founder, and pioneer of the Certified Cash Flow Specialist Designation, who introduced me to the term "cash flow" and her cash flow system, a value-based spending system. "Many financial gurus will attempt to tell you exactly what you should and shouldn't value and therefore how you should use your money. Advice like 'You shouldn't have two cars,' 'Give up your coffee in the morning,' 'Don't go on any family trips until your debt is paid off,' may not work for you. These opinions can sometimes cause the desired effect for the short term but not necessarily make it sustainable. Anytime someone gives you advice that doesn't align with your personal life values or your money mindset, the probability that you'll manage to make change and continue to progress toward your goal diminishes" (from her book, *Spent: Your Money Mindset Is the Key to Your Financial Freedom*).

Holmes-Winton created a specific cash flow system training that she now teaches to the financial advisory community. This system changed everything in my approach to our family money. I completed her Cash Flow Boot Camp in an attempt to stay current professionally and possibly find a few takeaways to pass on to my clients. I was excited to try this new financial method in our own house. My family members have always been my lab rats—I try to practise what I preach on them and then examine the outcome for what I can pass on. My daughters were in grade eight and grade six at the time, perfect ages to incorporate them into a family plan for our money. After six months, I was hooked. The scarcity-diet mentality that usually kicks in when tracking household money had flipped into an empowering abundant mindset approach that I could share and teach my children.

After the cash flow training, I felt as if the concept of

aligning my own individual life values to my spending was exactly the piece of the puzzle that I needed. What my family and I choose as important and necessary is going to be different from what others choose.

The more general financial term "value-based spending" refers to spending your money on those things that are truly important to you. Once you have set aside money for the crucial items first, like saving for your future self at retirement, emergency savings, and all the basic needs (food, shelter, etc.), then you can direct your financial resources so that your spending matches your values.

The Basics

The basic and general idea of cash flow planning is that you initially identify your priorities and your fixed expenses, such as retirement savings, insurances, household utilities, emergency savings, mortgages, loans, utilities, taxes, and so on. A vacation can be a fixed expense if the vacation falls into a priority list or it reflects your values. This will depend on the individual. Then a calculated remaining amount is left to spend on the things that you can control and that are variable, such as groceries, eating out, entertainment, clothing, hobbies, and coffees. This remaining spending amount is broken up into weekly cash amounts.

On my website at www.astrafinancial.ca, I have a cash flow worksheet for you to use to figure out your own cash flow.

In our house, every Sunday we transfer from our main bank account a specific amount to a separate bank account that we can access with a debit card. This amount is to last seven days. Because all our fixed bill payments and prioritised savings (for such as vacations, a new car, and renovations) are set up with the bank to happen automatically, we can fully spend our seven-day allowance how we choose guilt free. There is a specific calculation and a formula that helps you find what your seven-day allowance should be to meet all your needs and fund your wants.

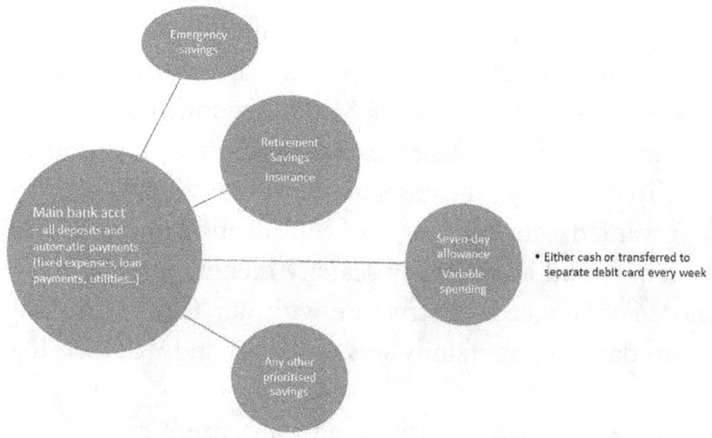

Getting Started

I remember calling a family meeting when I first wanted to introduce this system. I shared with my daughters that I wanted to include them in the planning. My older daughter, who was slouched on the couch, straightened up and leaned in close to ask, "Are we in money trouble? Do you have enough cash?"

I didn't mean to worry them. I shared that we had enough money but that I wanted to start a cash flow system to see how it would work so that I could then share it with my clients. Deep down though I knew that we needed this system ourselves. I have a tendency to fall into a scarcity mindset, and because of the nature of what I do for a living, I worry about having enough and making sure that we are saving enough.

I learned that it is a perfect solution for helping us manage and plan for extreme expenses. Both our daughters were competitive swimmers with our local swim team. At first, the costs were modest, but then as they swam faster and qualified for various national standards, the cost skyrocketed. We were paying $1,000 a month, not including the monthly travel expenses across Canada and into the US. That one year, the costs totalled close to $24,000.

I wanted a stronger sense of control and I knew that this system would alleviate my scarcity mentality and give me more confidence and structure with our family spending. From day one, my family was on board and we worked as a team.

Once we had allocated all our fixed expenses to automatic payments and our savings to automatic savings, I set us up with $600 a week to spend on groceries, eating out, personal expenses, clothing, and so on. This amount was for our entire family, not just for me.

It took us about three months to get the hang of it. One of the difficulties was that the $600 a week went to our debit card for both Ian and me to use; no extra cash was available in this account. Its sole purpose was for the weekly money only.

On day three of our family money plan experiment, I went to pay for groceries and house supplies but the store declined my debit card. I was embarrassed and livid at the same time. I immediately called my husband, already mad and demanding to know what he had spent money on. He let me know that he had picked up some groceries and he had had to run to Canadian Tire to get a gadget for his truck.

We learned immediately that good communication is vital for success in implementing this system. In the beginning, it is possible to feel resentful, because it can be difficult to have to always tell your partner if you are going to buy something. I had to make an effort to not criticize and sound accusatory. That first month was trial and error.

Sometimes, depending on the family money structure and relationships, I suggest to clients that they calculate a split so that each person has their own weekly cash amount.

Freedom

Personally, I have enjoyed the progression of communication with my husband and our teens. During routine family meeting check-ins, we evaluate how we have spent our $600 a week. Our mindset started to shift naturally, so that we subconsciously prioritized our purchases.

For example, one evening we had all come home late from work and school, and did not have any meal plan for supper. I asked everyone if they wanted to order take-out food. To my surprise, our daughters suggested that we make something from the fridge and pantry, and try to throw together some leftovers, because they would rather save up our money for a weekend family supper at a nice restaurant. Somewhere along the way our brains had happily switched to an abundance mode that left us happy making do with what we had around the house. They had chosen to prioritize spending on something that meant more to them at a later date.

Before our cash flow plan, we would have done both, ordered take out and dine out without thinking, and then I would have felt guilty after. In that moment, I knew that we were learning to appreciate and respect how we spend our money.

Soon after realizing the power and confidence we felt on a cash flow plan, we came up with a meal plan and a grocery plan. The positive effect was contagious and addicting. In our family meetings on Sundays, we plan our meals for the week. Everyone contributes and then our daughters go and get the groceries according to the menu. Prior to adopting our cash flow system, we would spend $500 a week at Superstore or Walmart making mindless random purchases for groceries. In my mind, that is too much money for only weekly groceries and is not an affordable lifestyle for our family. Looking back, it feels senseless and wasteful. Now, our family recognizes that if we can keep our grocery bill lower, then we can spend on other things that we choose—this is freedom.

Informed

I try to check my seven-day-allowance bank account a few times a day before I make a purchase anywhere. My husband checks our account as well before he has to buy something. Being a specific amount of money, it limits our family from overspending. It teaches us to spend with awareness and so we prioritise and match our spending to what is of true importance to us. Depending on the balance and if it is getting low near the end of our seven days, we will text to let each other know if we are making a purchase that will drastically deplete the debit card.

I shared this recently with a friend and she asked me, "Isn't it a pain to always have to check your bank account? I would rather use my credit card all the time."

Spending with purpose and forethought means taking stock of what cash is available to you and having the power of deciding if that spending matches your priorities. Without a way to quantify and qualify our spending, we can have a hard time recognizing our primary goals.

Using a credit card for everyday purchases had my family overspending. I had no accountability and no constraint. Yes, I may have paid the bill in full every month, but I still spent money meaninglessly and without purpose. In fact, every month when I paid the bill I was filled with angst, shame, and disbelief that we had spent so much. It did not feel good and the credit card bill would activate my scarcity mindset loop.

I have been asked, "Why would you give up all the credit card points? Credit card points are free money."

I calculated that we used to receive an average of fifty dollars' worth of credit card dollars a month by using our credit card. I have more than quadrupled that amount by the savings we have made by using our cash flow system and not overspending in the first place. I am actually ahead by ditching the idea of credit card bonuses.

Do you get that pit-in-the-stomach feeling if you have to check your bank account? I meet a lot of women who feel sick at the thought of coming face to face with the numbers on the screen. They are scared to open their mail because of bill phobia. They live in constant fear of scarcity and with a feeling of not having enough.

I suggest setting yourself up with a cash flow plan. Try it out. Allow your mindset to shift and take in the benefits of feeling in control. This will spread power to other parts of your life.

Why Seven Days of Cash?

During cash flow system training, I was asked to write down what I had spent in the last three days. I was very confident that I could accurately recite what my purchases had been and their total cost. After the exercise, I pulled up my online banking and was shocked to find that the number was far from the truth. I had underestimated what I had actually spent. That was only for three days. Can you imagine the miscalculation if I had tried to complete the same exercise for a thirty-day time frame, the length of time before a credit card statement is issued? Our brains can only hold so much information in short-term memory and the seven days is a manageable length of time to work with a cash allotment.

Big Change

In my drive to lead my family to financial balance and success, I discovered that planning the ins and outs of our money enhanced my marriage and my relationship with my daughters. Knowing where our money was going and why brought us together and on the same page.

We use the word "freedom" in our house often. It has come to be one of our family values. We translate it to represent the choices we gain by spending less. Six years ago, our abundance and freedom mindset was starting to initiate other conversations in our house like overconsumption, time management, simplicity, and sustainability.

Our daughters' competitive swimming had them commuting early mornings before school and late afternoons after school. We were not home until 7:00 p.m. every night for supper. Our life was busy and it felt chaotic. We had to schedule our free time just to recuperate. There is a certain perspective that comes from elite athletes and the families who support them. As parents we are witness to all of the sacrifices that athletes make. Friendships, relationships, free time, and social activities are all pushed aside to maintain a high level in sport. Our children recognized the sacrifices and made the choices willingly and happily on their own. We had all learned how to process the need to prioritize our lives.

It was at this stage in our life that we were ready to take the next jump into exploring our true family value of freedom, where freedom means more time, more options, and more ways to free up the clutter in our lives that was not important to us anymore.

We started the conversation of moving to a central location so that we could free up commuting time. I wanted the option of walking or riding my bike to work. I began reading a few books about simple living and sharing those books with my daughters. I will admit they panicked when I made them watch a documentary called *Tiny: A Story about Living Small.* It is a story of building a 120-square-foot home. My daughters made me promise that we would never do that.

Our home at the time had three living rooms and four bathrooms, if you counted the basement living space. Our large storage space in the basement included an empty plugged-in fridge and freezer. That space was packed full to the ceiling with boxes and junk; it was hard to walk in. We had so much space that we filled it with many unnecessary items that we never utilized or had the time to use. Those boxes had not been opened for over five years.

I asked my family what they thought of downsizing. The idea and conversation of downsizing took a year. It would be a big change but the timing was perfect. I knew that to leave my current firm to go solo and start my own financial planning firm would require a nest egg of start-up cash. Our family value was freedom and taking on debt to start a new firm would not feel like freedom.

After much discussion, my family was on board to downsize, to take on a very small mortgage while interest rates were low, and to use some of the cash from the sale of our house to ensure a nest egg of cash savings for my business. Our search then continued for the perfect small house. It had to have two bathrooms and not require renovations. After a year, we found a house and moved in. We were fortunate enough to have the means to buy the new small house and keep our original one until we could fully move and prepare to sell it. There was almost a six-month overlap of owning the two houses, which to us was worth every penny to not have to rush the move and the transition. It took that long just to come to terms with eliminating a lot of clutter and unnecessary items.

Our small home is a hundred years old and not quite 900 square feet in size. It has character and all new electrical and plumbing fixtures. We love the location close to Regina downtown in an area called Cathedral Village, where there are boutiques, shopping and restaurants. We are happy that we downsized and moved to a location that is minutes away from everything we need and do. We may have lost square footage, a garage, and our hot tub, but we have gained our family time, ease of commuting, and money.

Our downsizing has also sparked a simplicity transition. It started because we have to treat our house similarly to the way we treat our camping and hiking trips—pack out what you pack in. This is one of the principles for leaving no trace when you are in the wilderness and wanting to leave the outdoors as you found it. Our house does not have the space or storage to bring in unnecessary items. As extra items occasionally show up, we have to find a new home for them. This concept has helped to keep my shoe purchases to a minimum, my clothing to only my favourites and the essentials, and our kitchen gadgets down to bare bones. I no longer find the need to purchase unnecessary items and this mindset shift has carried on to our daughters.

We often comment that we can never go back to living anywhere else. But, let me be honest—there are days when we are all underfoot and driving each other crazy. That is when my husband comments that he misses his garage and I secretly wish for a glass of wine in my hot tub.

Our home is comfy and cozy, not glamorous. So, on top of the lack of space, occasionally there is an inner ego battle. Every once in a while, my ego demon kicks in and I want to move to a fancier area, with a brand new large house. Those days are few but when we have them, we talk about it, entertain the thought of buying a larger house, and then quickly dismiss it because of our one word, freedom. Knowing our own values makes our family decisions very easy and less stressful.

It is the same in my business. My business has a mission statement and a values system that I share with my staff. Our mission is to provide exceptional client service and advice. This is done through ongoing, proactive communication, education, and follow through. Our values are honesty and integrity, meaning that everything we do is in the best interests of our client. Any decision we make, we ask ourselves, "Is this for the good of our clients?" Our personal service and our commitment to bringing our honesty and integrity into every transaction makes for mutual trust and long-lasting relationships with our clients. With every decision we make in my business, whether in serving clients or accepting new clients or making a comprehensive business decision, I refer to our values of honesty and integrity and our vision of personal service. This eliminates hours, days, and weeks of grappling and questioning an outcome. This is the same system used in our family. We avoid a lot of pressure and stress by staying true to what we believe is the most important to us.

Everyone needs a system for cash flow. Whether it is the system that I shared with you or your own version, having a plan for your money is vital to your financial health.

In any cash flow system, there is a need to know how much you are spending and why you are spending that amount. Quantify and qualify the flow to take control of the flow. This will help you match your money to your own priorities and values.

At the end of the day, your cash flow system will help you automate your life so that you have less time to worry, feel more in control, and live life to the fullest.

What system do you have in place for spending and saving your money?

Chapter 6—Mapping the Family Financial Values System

"If you don't know where you are going, you might wind up someplace else."
Yogi Berra[10]

If you want to bring clarity to your money and your decisions then it is fundamental to understand what your priorities and your values are.

So what are your personal financial values? Simply put—your values represent what is important to you. They are the choices you make and why you behave the way you do. In this chapter there is integration among your meaning, your purpose, and your money.

Our values will help us grow and develop. Every day we make decisions that are a reflection of our values and beliefs and they are directed with a specific sense of purpose and meaning. The purpose is what is needed to bring a collective and collaborative approach to our lives. When our values are shared within a family, we build a positive, healthy, and thriving unit with the benefit of being able to prioritise effectively.

Having values and being able to define them will make life easier.

It's time to come alive with your own story, passion, and purpose. Here you will discover your own financial values and reorganize your relationship to money in order to support your vision.

Building Confidence from Chapter 1

The biggest financial barrier that I witness in women is that we can be champion self-doubters. Studies have shown that men are more likely than women to project confidence, and that women are particularly hesitant when being asked questions in a traditionally male-dominant environment.

In the first chapter, Tracy shared with me her experience with a pushy and domineering financial advisor. Based on fear, anxiety, and unease, Tracy made a financial decision that she later regretted. She told me that she had lacked self-confidence and power in that moment.

Maybe you have had a similar situation. This can be the motivation and drive to learn more and build the fortitude to take the reins. I believe that you can get where you want to, faster and with more ease, just by being able to ask more questions with sureness.

Financial security will mean different things to different people. It refers to the peace of mind that you feel when you are not worried about your money and future financial self. In my experience, financial security isn't about making a certain amount of money. There are many people who make millions of dollars who do not feel financially secure. Think of the superstar athletes and the multi-million-dollar lottery winners who claim bankruptcy. No amount of money made those people feel financially secure. However, there are multiple factors that align to help provide immunity around our money. Some examples of this might be striving to be debt-free, changing our money-belief system, being in control of expenses and spending, and consistently saving on a regular basis with a healthy and abundant attitude.

Reread the various definitions of financial empowerment in the last pages of chapter one. Women shared common themes around security, choices, following their dreams, and feeling good about money.

Your Definition of Financial Empowerment

Here is your chance to write your own definition of financial empowerment.

What does financial empowerment look like to you?

____

____

____

____

Are these beliefs still guiding you today?

____

____

____

____

Are there any beliefs you are ready to let go?

____

____

____

____

Remember when I shared with you that I have worked with people who make $30,000 a year and others who make $300,000 a year, and the money shame is the same for each? Everyone has some sort of money shame. You are not alone.

At the end of chapter two, I recounted Hannah's money shame story. She shared a story of guilt, jealousy, and shame. She writes, "Looking back, it is so clear to me why I have been terrified of financial success—it felt bad. It is so clear to me why I have found comfort being in debt—it ensured my place in the family."

Refer back to the money shame phrases in chapter two. At some point in our lives we have all heard these:

- Don't talk about money; it isn't appropriate.
- I am just not good with money.
- She is just not good with money.
- It's just way over my head.
- I am too creative and free-spirited to get a handle on it.
- We don't have two nickels to rub together.
- That's too rich for my blood.
- We can barely make ends meet.
- I should have more in the bank right now.
- Where does it all go?
- It takes money to make money.
- Money is the root of all evil.
- I don't deserve that; it costs way too much.

Your Chance to Change Money Shame Sayings

Do you believe any of these sayings?

____

____

____

____

What myth do you hear yourself say in your head? If so, write down the saying(s) you believe.

____

____

____

____

Cross these phrases out with your pen. Strike a line through each one. Now say these words aloud as you write, "I am enough, I have enough, and I am full of gratitude."

Now, take a deep breath. Forgive the past and give yourself permission to move on and heal.

Try this: with your eyes closed, take a deep breath and on your inhale say to yourself, "I forgive," and on your exhale say to yourself, "I release." Do this as many times as you need to and come back to this as often as you like.

The Power of Gratitude

I recently signed up for an online thirty-day gratitude challenge. Each day, I had to write one thing I was grateful for in work, my relationships, my body, and spiritually. By the second week, I felt a shift occurring in my mindset. I felt more joy, happiness, and positive emotions. Imagine if we can harness this feeling around our money emotions.

Robert A. Emmons, PhD, has carried out scientific studies that link gratitude with well-being. His research demonstrates that gratitude effectively increases happiness and can reduce depression. The practice of focusing on all that we have, rather than on what we don't have will help increase well-being and spark prosperous and abundant emotions.

Try placing your hands on your heart, close your eyes, and tell yourself as many times as you need, "I am enough, I have enough, and I am full of gratitude." Use this as your mantra.

Being grateful signifies that you acknowledge what you do have versus what you don't have.

Exploring Our Relationships from Chapter 3

One of the biggest causes of stress in relationships can be around money. Generally, we all have individual goals, values, and habits with money. Divergent views and values can make for tension in our relationships. Often partners have different saving and spending habits. Before we can align individual beliefs with a partner or a family member, we should become familiar with our own.

Your Relationship with Money

What does money mean to you? Write out at least four meanings.

____

____

____

____

Why do they mean that to you?

____

____

____

____

Refer back to chapter three where I shared a story about a couple I worked with. She was a saver, adamant that they not spend a dime, whereas he was more of a risk taker, wanting to take on more debt for a kitchen renovation and a new car. They fought and butted heads often and it was always about money.

The discussions in my office were getting heated. I asked each of them to reflect on their first money memory, the first time they could remember the concept of money.

She shared that her memory was of wearing a hand-me-down dress from Sears Bargain Center. She felt like there was never enough money. Her memory came from a place of scarcity and a fear of not having enough.

Her husband shared that he remembered taking coins from his parents' dresser. He came from a place of abundance because there was a plentiful supply of money and always enough to buy what he wanted.

It was then with tears in their eyes that they understood each other's money memory. Once they understood each other's story, they found respect and understanding. They began to communicate and appreciate each other more.

Your Family Financial Process

Do you know your partner's money story? How did you hear it?

____

____

____

____

What is it?

____

____

____

____

In your family, is there one person in charge of the finances, one seeing it as a burden, or one enjoying doing it? Write down your process.

____

____

____

____

Influencing Children's Approach to Money from Chapter 4

I often share with parents the Stanford University marshmallow experiment that I refer to in chapter four. It is a great lesson and reminder in delaying instant gratification. You can find clips on YouTube and watch the entertaining videos of children trying to avoid temptation and not eat the first marshmallow. This experiment is a fun way to remind ourselves that, with practice, we can train and build the habit of delaying instant gratification.

Whether we realize it or not, our childhood beliefs and thoughts have a tremendous impact on how we make decisions later in life. As parents, if we understand and are clear on our message, we can help to send a positive and healthy belief system to our children about money.

I have the opportunity now to look back and reflect on my life and the experiences that helped shape my belief systems. It is important to become aware of our personal history so that we can approach parenting with a foundation.

Your Money Lessons for Your Children

What lessons do you wish you had received as a child?

____

____

____

____

What message do you think you are sending to your children about money?

____

____

____

____

What do you want your child to learn?

____

____

____

____

What money system are you currently using or going to use to teach your children about money?

____

____

____

____

Putting Your Money Where Your Values Are through a Cash Flow System from Chapter 5

Your values are the motivators that give purpose to your money. Advice that screams “You can’t have your Starbucks coffee anymore” or “You shouldn’t take a vacation” comes from someone else’s belief set—it might not align with yours or your family’s. The concept of coordinating your own individual life values to your spending is vital to maintaining progress and sustaining a long-term strategy.

Our family uses a cash flow system that identifies and prioritises what is important to us. It is a communal effort that empowers every member of our family.

I shared in chapter five my family’s agreed-upon priority value is freedom. This means for us the choices we gain by spending less. Our family has downsized and simplified, all by choice, so that we can gain more time and more options in our lives. We avoid a lot of pressure and stress by staying true to what we value and believe are the most important elements in life to us as a collective.

Your family values will be different and unique from everyone else's. They will match what you decide is important to you, with your own answer as to why it is important.

I am a fan of Simon Sinek, author of *Start with Why: How Great Leaders Inspire Everyone to Take Action*. He has inspired a movement that asks, "Do you know your Why?" Your *Why* is the purpose, cause, or belief that inspires you to do what you do. This same concept should be applied with your money. When I meet with clients, we discuss why their money is invested the way it is, why they spend the way they do, why they save, and so on. Everything has a purpose with a why behind it.

Financial Purpose

We often talk about priorities in life, but how many of us have actually taken a moment to stop and write down our priorities on paper? Have you spent more time making a grocery list than you have spent writing down what is important to you and why?

The key is to identify the things that are most important to you at the core. You can have many values in life but you just need to discover the one or two that are your highest priorities.

So, let's map out your family values and why they are important to you.

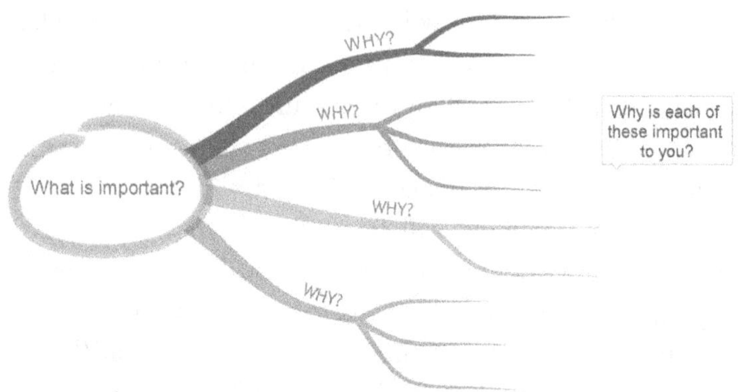

Here's how it works. On the left side of a piece of paper, write down the question, "What is important?" This can mean the same as asking yourself what makes you truly happy and brings you peace.

Start answering the question. There are no right or wrong answers here. This is where you have permission to bring everything important in your life to the conversation. Write down whatever comes into your head. Remember not to make any judgments at this stage. Just write everything down, no matter how strange, amusing, or scary! Feel free to add as many branches as you need.

Answer why each of those branches is important to you.

Now ask yourself again why each of these unique answers is important. Release any hidden deep-seated reasons and emotions you may recognize.

As an example, see Michelle's mind map. She chose "career" as an important branch. One of the reasons behind choosing "career" is her recognition of how much pleasure she equates with having a fulfilling income. Then, I asked her again, "Why is money important?" Her answer was "So I can take time away from work and be able to afford to spend it with my family."

Next step is to circle the words that come up more than once.

Michelle's mind map brought up the word "time" more than once. When I asked her if this felt true, she shared that this is her family's most important priority—spending time together.

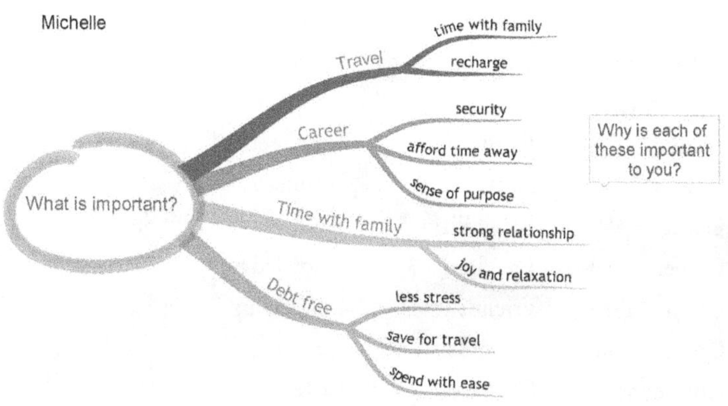

This mind map will help you build your values hierarchy. Each family member can complete it.

Here is a list of extended values that came up for some people. This list might help you make connections and insights into your own priorities.

Abundance	Contentment	Growth	Passion
Acceptance	Creativity	Happiness	Peace
Achievement	Empathy	Health	Prosperity
Adventure	Empowerment	Honesty	Purpose
Authenticity	Energy	Integrity	Recognition
Balance	Faith	Intelligence	Relationships
Beauty	Family	Intimacy	Respect
Caring	Flexibility	Kindness	Security
Career	Freedom	Knowledge	Spirituality
Clarity	Friendship	Leadership	Success
Compassion	Generosity	Learning	Truth
Confidence	Gratitude	Love	Wealth

Your Chance to Establish Family Financial Values

Plan a family meeting. Share, discuss, and talk about each of your mind maps. Record what takes place.

____

____

____

____

What values are similar?

____

____

____

____

What values will guide your financial decisions in your home.

____

____

____

____

How best can your money work to match your values?

____

____

____

____

Aligning

Your spending should be a reflection of what you truly value. However, it is common to fall out of step with what is important to you. This can happen slowly and over time if there is not a conscious effort to pay attention to where your money is going.

When I meet with people for cash flow planning, it is generally because they have a feeling of wandering with their spending. This can happen for a number of reasons—stress, a feeling of scarcity, and fear, or something as simple as being busy and not being mindful. No matter the reason, we all need a reboot.

Not long ago, I met with a single mom, Susan, who had fallen off course with her money. She had felt overworked, rushed, and was exhausted at the thought of checking her bank balances and statements. In our conversations, I learned that she felt lonely and then resentful that she had to be the sole caretaker of money. She didn't have a partner to help share the burden of managing the household finances. After the initial month of not being aware of her spending, she told me she was too overwhelmed to monitor her spending. She felt it was easier to just pay a lump sum on her credit card without reviewing the statement and examining it. Her lump sum was based on what she could afford, not what she owed. She confessed this went on for months because she knew it would just feel worse and worse to check her statements and confront the numbers. Previous to this slip up, she had paid off her bills in full every month and monitored her spending. In the past, she had felt in control and confident that her spending was conscientious and reflected what was important to her. When we met, she felt physically ill and was losing sleep at night.

As I said before, we all need a reboot. This happens to all of us. We are human and life takes over. The key is to nip the slippage in the bud early and get back to a place of awareness that feels positive and confident.

When Susan completed her values map, her main branch of importance was being debt free. She felt that being debt free would give her confidence and power that was essential to her as a single mother. Being debt free would eliminate her vulnerability. I asked her to open her bank statements and credit card statements. We reviewed her spending. Susan told me that her expenses reflected her loneliness. She had overshopped for clothing and gadgets that she realized she didn't need. When she reviewed her statements, she realized that her loneliness and resentment were dictating her finances and that her overspending was just adding fuel to that same fire. Her reboot has since been positive and allowed for a growing savings account.

Review your last bank and credit card statements. Compare your spending and saving with your values map. Is there a disconnect? Do you need to reassess and realign?

You are a work in progress and I suggest that you come back to your map every year and check in and review, noticing if there has been a shift in your alignment.

Change your story and you will change your life.

Now, rewrite your money story to be how you would like your relationship with money to be three years from now. Tell a new story and your life will follow the new direction.

Chapter 7—Making Your Money Work for You

"Wealth doesn't come from what you have. Wealth comes from what you DO with what you have."
Barbara Stanny[11]

Every money decision you make right now should fulfill your mission and vision. What you spend on, where you save, and how much you save are all related to your WHY.

Use your money as fuel to ignite the things that mean the most to you. Controlling your money story starts here. This is the beginning of your money destiny.

What you need to know about making your money work for you:

- It is simpler than you think.
- It doesn't consistently take a lot of your time.
- You don't need a lot of money to create more money; you just need to create a habit.
- It is never too late to start.

Knowledge and confidence are going to strengthen

your financial picture. This chapter will capture the framework you need to build knowledge around your money.

Taking Action and Getting Started

Money In and Money Out

Tracking how much you put in your bank account each month and then how much you spend will bring on a triage of emotions. I will often do this exercise and feel really negative about some of the spending. I usually scream inside my head, "Really? That much on take out and eating out!" But, this is the first step to truly regaining your power and taking control. I know that this might be the last thing that you want to do and it is usually the hardest, but it is vital to measure and track how you are doing. This is the only way to improve—quantify and measure.

First, write down your fixed monthly expenses. Remember in chapter five, I shared my family's cash flow planning and directed you to a cash flow worksheet on my website www.astrafinancial.ca. Part of the cash flow planning process was identifying fixed expenses. These are the bills that have to be paid and are part of your basic necessary living like utilities, mortgage, phone (not groceries), etc., and don't forget the expenses that happen less frequently, like auto insurance and annual payments. If your fixed expense fluctuates slightly, assume the highest average of the monthly fixed expense.

You will need to look at your debt. Just a quick note on the terms "good debt" and "bad debt." I refer to "bad debt" as borrowing money to purchase something that you consume and use up quickly or something that depreciates in value. "Good debt" is something that you use to purchase an asset that will appreciate and grow over time, or be sold for a profit. Is there a need to add debt repayment to your fixed expenses? Is there an outstanding credit card balance or a loan owing? Perhaps one of your family values is to be debt free and pay off your loan and credit card? Acknowledge that repayment and add it to your fixed expenses. Perhaps travel is one of your family values. Or maybe saving to create a side business that you love is one of your family's main values? Whatever it is you identified in your financial values map as a priority needs to be added as an additional fixed expense side bucket.

Then, write down your monthly income. For some, this will be an easy set monthly amount that doesn't change. Others may have a sporadic income that changes over the course of a year (for example, business owners including those who are self-employed); they will have to calculate a best estimate.

Calculate whether your income is enough to meet your expenses. This might be a hard exercise for you; it might leave you feeling very negative and as though you are coming from a place of scarcity. Recognize these feelings, whatever they may be, and acknowledge that you have the power and are gaining the knowledge to create positive change. This is a huge step.

The remaining amount is left to spend on the things that you can control and that are variable—groceries, clothing, entertainment, etc. This is where using weekly cash for your variable spending works really well.

Simplifying

While you are exploring and tracking your money, you will be able to see the bank fees or any extra charges that might be unnecessary. Do you have several bank accounts squirreled away in different locations? Are there monthly fees at each of them? This can bring the realization that you need to simplify your money. How many credit cards are you using? Why? Do you have investment accounts in multiple locations?

As much as we say we need simplicity and clarity, we are very good at choosing complexity. Somehow there is an association of complexity meaning superior or somehow better. The level of complexity in the financial services arena has grown in options whether they are mortgages, credit cards, or investments. Every year, hundreds of new financial products are rolled out. Let me tell you, overcomplicating a thing does not provide it with higher quality.

Almost all my clients come to me to consolidate and simplify their investment life. There is no purpose or meaning in their having five different banking or investment accounts. But, having a specialist like me coordinate their accounts brings purpose to their money. By consolidating and simplifying, we can plan and structure a person's investments to match their retirement needs and their tax planning. We provide an overall big-picture coaching. We then guide our clients how best to diversify their investments in different companies.

Chapter 7

Lynn's Story of Simplifying

My client Lynn and I had been talking about business, life, and the importance of simplifying. I asked her to share with me her shift toward a life of meaning and ease.

"It was eleven years ago. I was a corporate strategic planner working for a company that was in the throes of a merger. My job tripled in one year, but my staff, nor the expectations placed upon me, had not. My daughters were teenagers then, and my husband was working out of town and only home on weekends. I felt like I had been swallowed whole, and I am claustrophobic. I remember the day that I sat in front of my boss and told him that life—my job and the demands placed on me—was not sustainable. That was the first time I heard myself admit that I was fallible.

"I knew I had to make a change. Alter my reality. Walk against my own traffic. Venture into unknown territory. But how?

"As a strategic planner, I did what came naturally. I devised a process to undertake this change and a timeline of one year with a single goal to identify those things that no longer served me so that I could begin the change process.

"Everything was on the table. My job. My personal relationships. My body. My relationship with food. My hair. My life. I set in place four principles as a guide: to commit three acts of defiance; to listen and seek to understand; to practice imperfection; and to avoid rooms with no doors.[12]

"During that year, I changed my hair and my job and I became better at saying no. I adopted healthy practices that continue to serve me to this day—including embarking on a regular exercise program for which I am now a fitness instructor, and changing my diet to exclude foods that do not make me feel good, including dairy, meat, and processed foods.

"But beyond, bigger shifts were happening 'underground' that I was not aware of, but would come to reveal themselves over the next eleven years; they continue. I left my corporate career for entrepreneurship, which opened up a world that I always envisioned someday. I published my first book—*How to Be a Pink Flamingo in a Brown Duck Pond*; created a publishing company that publishes *SKY Magazine* , a publication that is dedicated to entrepreneurship and fashion; created my own consulting company (Lynear Thinking) to help entrepreneurs think and do great things; and became the owner of the shoe boutique, ZÖE, that has literally carried me through all the steps of my own life.

"Practically every aspect of my life changed, how I view time, and my money story. I went from spending time at things that were soul killing and spending for placation to spending my time on soul-filling work and investing, and indeed being mindful and respectful of money and its part in the achievements of my life and business goals."

Lynn Armstrong is the author of *How to Be a Pink Flamingo in a Brown Duck Pond*. She is a local magazine publisher of SKY and the owner of ZÖE shoe boutique. Connect with her at www.lynnlarsonarmstrong.com.

Your Buckets

Your money should have landing spots—buckets to land in; each bucket must serve a purpose for you. These buckets should become a part of your fixed expenses.

Here are some of the most important buckets.

Savings Account

The goal for your savings account should be to carry a positive balance with an amount that can cover the additional, unplanned-for monthly expenses that come up. I am thinking of the surprise speeding ticket expense I had last month, or the extra school fee that your kids brought home for their outdoor education trip. That list goes on and on with surprise expenses. This is where a savings account can come in to cover those expenses.

The undesirable alternatives for some people with few financial resources are using the credit card, taking out a payday loan, or borrowing from friends and family. We should try to avoid those alternatives.

Deciding the amount that you would like to have in your savings account is a personal decision. I have worked with clients who feel comfortable with a $1,000 balance, a $5,000 balance, all the way up to a $100,000 balance. Everyone has their own sweet spot and reason for anchoring on a dollar amount.

The individual with a $1,000 goal in a savings account is a young professional who does not have many expenses and lives a very modest lifestyle. A thousand dollars feels like a safe amount to cover the additional expenses that might occur.

The couple who is comfortable with $5,000 in a savings account uses that amount because it is the minimal amount that the bank requires for a no-fee account with unlimited transactions. Their savings account goal is to always maintain that balance and to never go below it so that they avoid incurring fees.

The couple with $100,000 in a savings account are in their sixties. They are a ranching family that raises cattle and also farms the land. They feel anxious and very stressed when their savings account dips under this amount. If there is an equipment failure, a building repair that must be done, or a payroll emergency, they need the liquid cash immediately to keep their operation going. Because of their past experience this need happens regularly.

Emergency Bucket

Regardless of a family's income, there is always the possibility that a wage earner could become ill, injured, or unemployed. How will the bills be paid? There is also the possibility of a large catastrophic expense. We have all heard the story of a friend who had a vehicle transmission or motor die. The vehicle was no longer under warranty, considered worthless, and yet it still needed replacement. Recently, a friend of mine had a basement repair that was necessary and immediate. Her house was sinking and the foundation needed major construction. The cost to repair it was $40,000.

The emergency bucket is separate from your savings account. Having money in reserve is an important goal for every family and individual. It brings peace of mind that there is a back-up plan if needed. Interest rates are historically low, but that shouldn't deter you from building up your emergency stash. The point of this bucket is not to treat it as an investment. With that said, you can look for a higher interest cash savings account, but try not to get hung up on making interest on this money.

In the beginning you may feel overwhelmed in trying to build this nest egg. You have heard all of us financial experts talk about needing three months' expenses saved, or three to six months of your income saved. We do need a goal of an amount to anchor on and work towards, but do not get stressed about that amount. It may feel discouraging to try to save six months' income while also trying to live on your current income. So, take baby steps. Just start. Find an amount that fits in with your cash flow plan to allocate to an emergency savings account that is out of sight. It will take some time to build this. Just stay the course and continue the habit.

Retirement Savings

"Bag lady worry" is a real thing. I often meet women who are truly worried and scared that they will be homeless bag ladies having to eat cat food. The fear is usually triggered by a lack of confidence and a lack of knowledge about their financial circumstances. Panic and a sense of paralysis can easily set in if there is no way to distinguish and filter out the noise from the financial media. How often do you hear in the news the latest report released claiming that to retire you need a million dollars or some new calculated formula? That is enough to scare anyone who doesn't have a clear grasp of their own financial picture. Do not rely on what a news outlet reports for the general masses.

My role as an advisor to my clients is to help educate, coach, and plan so that their fears can be addressed and flipped to assurance in their own financial position and their personal needs.

We are going to tune out the big-numbers talk right now and defer questions like, "How much should I have so I can retire?" Instead we will concentrate on right now, this moment that you have control over. What amount in your cash flow right now can you save for your future self? That is where you start. In the next chapter, I talk about finding expert advice to help you dig deeper with the numbers you need later in life. For now, we will focus on getting started.

Out of your cash flow you should be allocating some money towards your retirement savings—your future self. You have a few choices of what bucket to use.

Registered Retirement Savings Plan (RRSPs)

This is meant to be used for longer-term savings that will grow until you decide to retire and start withdrawing money. Initially, your RRSP contribution is tax deductible. When you do withdraw money, it is considered taxable income to you. However, as you save and contribute to the RRSP, you can reduce the amount of income tax you pay in that year.

Tax Free Savings Account (TFSA)

The TFSA is a Canadian account that you can save in and not have to declare any income when you withdraw the money. Also, there are no tax implications on any growth. However, the contributions to a TFSA are not deductible for income tax purposes, unlike contributions to an RRSP. I believe the best use for your TFSA is to use it for long-term savings. The growth and interest you can make over the long term will help supplement your retirement income without having to pay tax.

I have met people who started a TFSA at the bank in a so-called "high interest account" that made them only 0.05% interest. This defeats the benefits of the account, because a TFSA is meant to shelter the most growth and interest possible. Such a low interest as 0.05% does not keep up with the rate of inflation, which in Canada in 2016 was 1.7%. Be sure to utilize the advantage with this account. Because growth and interest in a TFSA are not taxed, this account is the perfect place to invest in equities for the long term, similar to your RRSP.

The other mistake that is common people make is to use their TFSA as a revolving door for expenses. The government has a limit that accumulates each year and tracks what amount you have contributed and what amount you have withdrawn. Because you have to wait until the following year to contribute back the amount you withdrew, there is the potential to over-contribute in a year. There is some tracking that needs to be monitored and I am positive that the bank is not going to stop and question your limits if you are constantly putting in and taking out. On my advice, my clients treat the TFSA as an RRSP and part of a longer-term strategy for their future selves.

Generally, a combination of these two retirement savings buckets—RRSPs and a TFSA—is a fantastic way to save for your retirement personally. The amount to save in either the RRSP or the TFSA will be dependent on your current tax bracket and your future tax bracket at retirement.

I specifically remember my first RRSP purchase. It was

not as exciting as my first kiss but I remember feeling just as young and foolish, not knowing anything. I was twenty-five years old and that year my husband and I owed income tax. Someone had told us that we could either pay the Canada Revenue Agency $2,000 or purchase an RRSP and keep the money. So we marched straight to the bank to contribute to an RRSP. This was my first experience with investing. We came up with some money and transferred $3,000 to an RRSP. Quick and easy. In and out. No one discussed an ongoing savings plan, whether we thought we would owe taxes again the next year, what we should be investing in, and if we had a plan for the future. There was no spark or recognition of, "Hey, this should be an ongoing thing. You should be saving monthly." We were not making very much money. I was staying home to raise our daughters. We were spending every penny we made. Owing extra money at tax time felt crippling. We could have used good advice and money coaching at that time, but it was a start and an initial introduction to the idea and awareness of needing to start saving money for our future selves and our taxes.

Pensions

Hopefully, your employer has a pension plan that you can contribute to directly from your paycheque. The amount that you contribute is an out-of-sight-and-out-of-mind saving, meaning that because it is automatically deducted from your pay, you can't spend it. Your employer will contribute as well and the benefit is that over time and during your working years, the savings will grow.

There are a couple of different types of pensions.

A Defined Benefit Pension Plan provides retirement income based on a formula that is a combination of years and salary. These plans are typically offered by the government and a very few private sector employers. Your retirement income might be based on a formula of 1.5% or 2% per year of service multiplied by a five-year average of your annual earnings at your best rate of income. Your employer takes on the investment risk with this type of pension plan, because no matter the market risk, you will be paid your retirement income for your lifetime.

The other pension is called a Defined Contribution Pension Plan. Your employer matches your contribution up to a certain level. A common example of a defined contribution plan is where you contribute 5% of your annual income and your employer matches with a 5% contribution; the contribution generally occur each paycheque. With this plan you carry the risk of the performance over your lifetime of the investments you choose. The amount of your retirement income is unknown and not guaranteed.

Regardless of which pension plan you have with your employer, it may very well be your greatest financial asset over time.

To Contribute or Not?

Mitch was a young man when he started working full time thirty years ago. He started as an inventory clerk, replenishing the shelves at the parts department of his local store. He stayed with the same employer and eventually moved to various other roles in the company, but he enjoyed his role as a sales rep at the counter. He made a modest income of an average of $55,000 gross salary a year. When Mitch originally started working, his employer asked him whether he wanted to join the contribution pension plan with the option of buying company stock directly from his paycheque. At the age of twenty-five, he chose to contribute to the pension plan and in addition automatically have the amount come off his pay to buy $25 worth of stock a month. He did this his entire career.

The other story is from Bob. He started his first job at age twenty-five as well. Bob's employer offered him a similar pension plan option, but Bob declined because he didn't want his paycheque to be less. He thought at the time, "I have plenty of time to think about retirement." Ten years went by and he finally decided to start contributing to his pension.

Both stories started off the same where each man began working at a very young age with their employer. They were both at entry-level jobs and not making very much to start with. They both stayed with the same employer for thirty years. Their story then takes a drastic turn. Mitch, who contributed from day one to a pension plan, has accumulated almost a million dollars because of his pension and his ongoing options to buy stock. But Bob is going to have to continue working because his pension will not be enough to retire on. He missed out ten years of free contributions and ten years of compounding interest from his employer.

The power of compounding interest over time and continuous savings is phenomenal. And then add in a matching "free" contribution from your employer. If your employer asked you if you would like a raise for several thousand dollars, would you say no?

Registered Savings

RRSP

Refer back to the entry on RRSPs under "Retirement Savings."

Registered Education Savings Plan

If you have children, you may decide that one of your priorities is to save for their education. If your cash flow can allow for it, I recommend taking advantage of the government matching grants in a Registered Education Savings Plan (RESP) by starting to save what you can afford. Just like all other savings, the earlier you start the better.

RRSPs versus RESPs

What if you truly don't have enough cash flow each month to contribute to both your retirement savings (RRSPs) and at the same time your children's education fund (RESP)?

You need to look after your future self and save today for yourself first. Of course, you value education and you love your children. The reality is that if you can only afford one, you are better off taking care of your own savings first. We do not want to be financial burdens to our children later in life because we did not take care of our own financial needs and savings. The reality of moving in with your adult children because you do not have sufficient retirement savings is not ideal.

Yes, student loans don't feel good and are a concern for young people, but your children will have youth and time on their side. You will be there to help guide them and share in financial literacy to make the right decisions to mitigate their debt and come up with a financial plan when they have completed their post-secondary training. The best thing you can do is sustain your own financial security and lead by example.

Insurance

This book has been about putting power into your own hands and creating confidence and empowerment with your money. But, unfortunately we have to address the uncontrollable, unpleasant what-if scenarios and ensure your power defensively. Protecting your family and talking about your own mortality is not fun. In fact, there is often resistance to addressing this situation. No one wants to imagine themselves not here and not with family. Young people are hesitant because they think they have all the time in the world. Remember when you were twenty and you thought forty-year-olds were old?

Insurance is meant to provide income replacement to your family if you were to die. One of your buckets should be a personal term life insurance policy. The best time to address your mortality with insurance is when you are young. Insurance pricing is based on your age and health. The younger you are, the cheaper it is. By the time you feel like you need it, the pricing is too expensive.

If anyone in your life is dependent on you, then you need life insurance. That includes children, spouse, parents, and other family members. The question to ask yourself is, "If I were to die tomorrow, would my family members be able to take care of themselves?"

If you stay home with children and you think that because you have no income then you have no need for insurance, you are wrong. Who is going to help raise your family? Will your family need to hire childcare, find someone to drive children to their activities, and so on. These are unpleasant thoughts, but if addressed properly, you can move on and know that you are protecting your family against the uncontrollable. That in itself is powerful and should put your mind at ease.

There are different types of insurance but the simplest and the least expensive is term insurance. Term insurance is a better choice over bank-offered mortgage insurance. It covers you for a specific length of time (twenty years) and is renewable or can convert to different types of insurance. Remember when I said that overcomplicating something does not equal higher quality? Well, this is true in insurance. There are so many complicated and confusing insurance products. For most us, they are too confusing and a waste of time and money. Start with term insurance.

Critical Illness Insurance

I am always hesitant with insurance products. I like to do my homework and investigate all products. Only when there is a need and a necessity do I recommend insurance. Critical Illness Insurance is one that I often recommend. It is a lump sum that is paid to you if you are diagnosed with a major illness. It is intended to cover any expenses that you face, like time off work, medical treatments, or unexpected travel. You spend the money as you see fit.

As you can imagine, the financial burden can be devastating if you become ill. Our provincial health care won't look after our personal finances, and short-term disability payments with your employer eventually run out. We all know of friends and family who have been diagnosed with an illness and survived. Fortunately with modern medicine, the survival rate is growing. I have been witness to Critical Illness Insurance policies being paid to clients. The money has brought peace of mind and a sense of control. Again, the best time to purchase this is when you are young and healthy. You can pay a level premium and own the policy until the age of sixty-five and there is the option that, if you did not need to make a claim, you can have all of your premium payments paid back to you.

Carly and Her Buckets

Carly, one of the women I interviewed, is a single professional who has taken care of her "buckets" and is living life to the fullest. She shared this with me.

> "Me, myself, and I. I'm single and fear that I might not find the frog that changes into my prince when I kiss him, so if I have to be in this life independently, I want finances to not be an issue for me. I've ensured I've covered all the basics: savings, insurance, my death. By taking these steps, I am comforted in knowing I've done my best to set myself up for my future and for my family."

Chapter 7

Debt

Debt can spark some of our money shame feelings. There is often a media release from national surveys that Canadian household borrowing has reached its peak. As I write this, Statistics Canada has released a statement that Canadians continue to accumulate debt, and households now owe an average of $1.68 for every dollar of disposable income.

When I initially meet with clients, we complete a total financial strategy and picture that provides them with guidance for their money decisions. We not only address investments but we bring purpose to their money. That purpose brings opportunity and acknowledges the money shame that might creep in. I have witnessed the transformation in confidence and happiness when my clients reduce their debt.

Yes, we need to curb our appetite for debt. And yes we need to talk more openly about money. But, we need to address debt on a personal level and from the heart. When you went through your fixed expenses and added debt repayment, you were looking at the big picture, your picture. You weren't reading the latest Statistics Canada release and adjusting your debt repayment based on fear messages. You were basing your payments on what you felt comfortable with and what you can afford. Just practising these steps will help instigate the pendulum swing in the right direction with an awareness going forward to match your money with your own personal family values. You will find that you will be more financially savvy about taking on any extra debt in the future.

Be gentle with yourself. Tune out the outside noise. Remember that you are enough and you have enough.

Chapter 8—Creating Your Dream Team aka Your Tribe

"A tribe is a group of people connected to one another, connected to a leader, and connected to an idea. For millions of years, human beings have been part of one tribe or another. A group needs only two things to be a tribe: a shared interest and a way to communicate."
Seth Godin[13]

Our exploration in this book has been to harness your power and your confidence while you steer your family money to do great things for you. Along the way, I hoped you learned that loving yourself is the first priority. Yes, you are this amazing being who is rocking life and doing it all, but self-love and self-respect must come before all life's other priorities. We can't give what we don't have. Our own self-care creates happiness and creates a flow that shares abundancy with your family and the world. Your own financial journey requires you to love yourself, be easy on yourself, and nurture your own needs.

You may have explored many internal barriers in the

early chapters. These barriers might sneak up and come back. They may need your affection and tender care to silence and move through. Listen to the wisdom of your wise self—your true inner voice that created your vision and purpose during this journey. Effective change requires effective involvement, meaning that you don't have to do this on your own. Part of your self-love is finding your tribe. Surround yourself with the right people, the people who are going to lift you higher and support you. We all need a trusting community.

Where do you get your money advice from? Does it come from a friend who you think is money smart, maybe a parent or a co-worker? Your money advice should come from a professional who can step back from the emotional side of money. As we travelled through the previous chapters, we learned that money is full of emotion and can affect our decision-making. That is why we need expert advice and coaching to be in our best interest. I like to think of myself as a financial mentor, one who shares past mistakes, stories, accomplishments, and expert advice. I push my clients to participate. The reward is not only success but personal growth, healing, and power.

I often talk with people who, after learning about what I do for a living and hearing me speak with passion about financial awareness and literacy, ask me to review their investments and financial decisions. I then ask if they already have a financial planner and they tell me, "Yah, I have an advisor guy that does my investments but I don't really like him or trust him and we never talk about anything else. Can you check my stuff and make sure it is in my best interest?"

Really? You don't trust the guy who handles all your money? Should this person really be on your team? Would you hand over your child to a babysitter you did not trust? This is a sign that you have not found the right tribe member yet. You need someone you can trust and who talks to you about the entire big picture. You deserve someone who will have your back and bring out the best in you. Stay with me here, keep reading, and I will give you some direction for finding the right member of your team.

Today is an era of distrust and outrage. And rightly so. They make movies about the wealth and carnage in the financial industry. Have you watched *The Wolf of Wall Street or The Big Short?*

Who Is Who among Your Troops

This is what you need to know as you assemble your troops, your dream team, your tribe.

Certified Financial Planner

This is a professional designation granted by the Financial Planning Standards Council in Toronto, Ontario.

Financial Advisor

This is an individual who renders financial services and advice. "Financial Advisor" is a broad term that is generally used to refer to almost anyone providing financial advice. It is not a professional designation that adheres to required examinations, training, and a code of ethics.

A Financial Planner

A Financial Advisor can call himself a "Financial Planner." That is confusing because he may or may not be certified. The term "planner" is not yet regulated in Canada.

When it comes to finding a trustworthy financial planner, you are at risk. You would think that everyone presenting themselves as a financial planner is certified, qualified, competent, and ethical. But, that is not the case.

Currently, as I write this in 2017, anyone offering financial advice can call themselves a financial planner. The term is unregulated and this leaves you vulnerable. There are approximately 80,000 individuals in Canada whose only qualifications are related to selling products. However, a Certified Financial Planner (CFP) must adhere to rigorous testing, accreditation, and standards, and has a written obligation to put the client's interests ahead of their own.

Ensure the member of your financial team is a certified financial planner, accredited with the Financial Planning Standards Council. You can check at www.fpsc.ca/find-a-planner-certificant as to whether your financial advisor is accredited.

Regulation of the financial services sector in Canada is slowly changing. Progress is happening. At a snail's pace, but it is happening. The Financial Planning Standard Council is trying to change the regulatory model so that only Certified Financial Planners can use the term "Financial Planner." The education and professional standards of a Certified Financial Planner are strict and they uphold individuals to professional standards and ethical behaviour. This is someone that you need on your team; you don't need a sales advisor.

When people approach me and tell me they don't like or trust their current advisor, it's because there is a little intuitive voice inside them that has picked up on the fact that their relationship with that person may be based on purchasing their products. Listen and acknowledge that voice inside you. Does this person on your team have your best interest at heart?

Compensation Matters

How your financial planner is compensated matters. The way a financial professional is compensated may affect the quality of service they deliver. If you ask your financial advisor how they are compensated and the explanation is too complicated to understand, then put on your runners and bolt. Someone might appear to be offering a free service since you never see the fee, but rest assured, nobody works for free. It is important to know the different styles of compensation so that you make an informed decision and have all of the information when you choose this member of your tribe. You want to find someone who puts your needs first.

Some advisors are tied to their company's products. Depending on where they work or what institution they are affiliated with, an advisor may only be able to provide you with their company's products. The affiliated product is not always apparent and can have a separate company name but still be a part of the parent company. Ensure you ask and research that there is no affiliated mutual fund or other product tied to the company that your financial professional works for. If your advisor is at a bank, they will be paid their salary plus a bonus for any sales that are tied to investment holdings and bank products.

Some investment products provide a commission to your advisor as soon as you make a purchase. If you use a stock broker, each trade may pay a commission. Mutual fund companies pay the advisor a few different ways.

The Front End Compensation to the advisor is generally 1% paid in twelve one-month instalments by the mutual fund company. The advisor is compensated from the management fee of the mutual fund. As an investor, you will not see this fee as it is paid by the mutual fund company.

The Deferred Sales Charge (DSC) is 5% to 7% paid upfront to the advisor from the mutual fund. The advisor is compensated from the management fee of the mutual fund company, and you do not see this either. However, if you change the fund or withdraw the money before a set period of time (five to seven years), you pay a DSC fee that comes right off your investment holding value. This can be very limiting.

It may be tempting for an advisor to suggest you switch your products often, regardless if there is a need or not to make a change, or to choose an appropriate product because of a large commission. In the investment world, this is known as churning. With a large percent paid to the advisor, one wonders if it is in the best interest of the client or not. The trust factor goes down. This was the most common form of compensation in the 1980s, 1990s, and early 2000s. I still see accounts that are based on this model.

The asset-based fee model is set as a percentage of a client's portfolio. If you had a $100,000 portfolio with an annual 1% fee, each year $1,000 is deducted from your investment account for advice and execution. The charge is transparent, so clients see this figure in writing and it is separate from product-based commissions. The amount is usually deducted at the rate of one twelfth of the fee every month. The mutual fund company does not compensate the advisor and the mutual fund fee is much less. Therefore, you generally pay a smaller overall fee with this model.

A fee-based advisor will charge for their service the same way a lawyer does—either by the hour or by the task.

For example if you want an advisor to put together a comprehensive financial plan, they might charge you at $200 per hour and work ten hours for a total of $2,000. Or they might have packages so you can pick how much service you want for a pre-determined price. This type of payment plan can be very useful, since you can hire the advisor when you need them and you know there is no product selling. Most people do not need a comprehensive financial plan drawn up for them every year and so this often works out as being better value than the yearly service fee.

So how do you know who to trust? You want someone you can depend on, someone you know is not going to gouge you with large fees. You can find some reassurance in knowing exactly how they are compensated. Any of the compensation models may work for you, as long as you understand exactly what you're paying and what you get in return.

Everyone needs a financial plan to start. Before my own firm accepts a new client, we have to complete a fee-based financial plan. Otherwise, how are we going to know anything about the individuals—their dreams, goals, finances, previous experiences, and misconceptions? What do you want? Why? These all need to be explored before you can decide how to invest your savings.

This is a lot of information to take in. My purpose in writing it for you is so that you can come back to it as needed. It is your reference point as you need it. As time goes on, it will make sense and the pieces will start to come together. As you search for your tribe and build it, your knowledge will grow and so will your experience.

The Search Begins

Now, it's time to start looking. Start asking your friends, family, and colleagues for references. Then research yourself. Your friends are not financial planners and they may not have the knowledge base to refer someone qualified and excellent to you, but they are a good place to start; then do your own due diligence.

As part of your questions, ask your friends whether they received a written financial plan, what did it cover, and did they have to pay for it. You should ask them how their advisor is compensated.

As I said above, you can verify the status of individual financial advisors and planners on the Financial Planning Standards Board (FPSB) website at www.fpsc.ca/find-a-planner-certificant. The site hosts a directory and registration of all Certified Financial Planners, and for each professional, it provides records on disciplinary history and the status of their designation. Before you choose your financial advisor, make sure that their designation is held in "good standing," and that they have no history of disciplinary action.

Then start interviewing the financial planners. Phone first, introduce yourself, ask what services they offer, and what they charge. You should then schedule an introductory meeting only if you are comfortable with the services and understand the fees.

Here is a list of questions to ask at your first meeting:

1. What are your qualifications?
2. Are you a certified financial planner?
3. What experience do you have? (Experience is important as is specific specialized training and experience.)
4. What services do you offer? (Services can vary depending on expertise and the organization that a financial planner is affiliated with.)
5. What is your approach to financial planning?
6. Is there a holistic, overall approach with your firm?
7. How will I pay for your services? (This should be disclosed in writing.)
8. Who besides me benefits from your recommendations?
9. Are there any affiliated products?
10. What education and financial literacy do you provide to your clients?
11. Can I have all these answers in writing?

Also as important is chemistry. Do you feel comfortable with this person? Will your financial professional take the time to understand your needs and help educate you. It is important to work with someone who understands the importance of your money story and your relationship with money.

Donna's Story

I remember when I first met Donna a few years back. She told me that she had left all of the financial decisions to her husband. When he passed away, she felt as if she had no idea how to manage. She phoned me on the insistence of her friend whom I had worked with.

Donna's financial knowledge started at ground zero. I could have glazed over everything, taken control, and managed her finances for her. That is the easy thing to do with someone who feels overwhelmed and trusts you. Instead, I took my time, we talked often, and I explained the whys and hows with her.

As I have said before, my role is to be a financial mentor and help teach financial literacy with participation. This method builds confidence and empowers individuals.

I remember that first year at tax time when Donna brought in a large box of papers and we dumped it on the table and spent an hour or two sorting it out before I could put it together for her accountant. I am proud to say that today she sorts it out, packages it, and even delivers it to the accountant herself. She came beaming into the office to let me know the first time she had completed it herself. This may seem like a very simple exercise, but for Donna this was a pivotal moment in her life. She sat back and during our coffee she said she was proud of herself, she felt in control, and she was starting to heal and find happiness again. This is the power of financial confidence with a supportive tribe.

Chapter 8

Good Advice

Why is it so hard to find good advice? There are a few reasons. Canada's financial industry is still run by pale, male, grey-haired advisors who started in this business thirty years ago, when most advisors were product and investment salesmen. Don't get me wrong, they provided a service and Canadians benefited by learning to save and accumulate over time. Imagine, Registered Savings Plans were only introduced in 1957 to promote savings for retirement. It was a relatively new thought to save for your own future after working. So, the 1980s' and the 1990s' model of financial advice was only a result of "the way things were."

But, it is time to acknowledge that times have changed and there is a higher expectation. I have been to meetings and seminars full of thirty or forty advisors over the age of sixty, disputing and fighting the changing regulations. The new regulations are being proposed to protect consumers, people like you, from having to pay hidden fees and commissions. I think this is great, but the financial advisory world of old school advisors are fighting this.

The line of trust starts to get blurry around the compensation models that advisors receive. In brokerage firms (selling stocks), each time an advisor buys or sells shares, their clients must pay them a fee for executing the trade. If you work at a brokerage, there is a sliding scale that changes every year, making it harder for advisors to make their revenue target mark—meaning to maintain their salary and bonus they have to sell more and make more trades every year. How is this in any way in the best interest of the client?

People are tired of having to weed out the noise and become their own advocate. I know that you may feel distrust and outrage. But stay with me … I believe there is something radical happening. There is a development—a movement, a revolution—that is honest and authentic amidst the noise. The financial advice world is starting to shift to a place of authenticity and meaning. There are financial planners like me who want to make a difference.

Attracting Other Members to Your Tribe

Be mindful about who you would like to attract into your tribe. What are the qualities you are looking for? On my path to creating financial confidence, I like to surround myself with people who are supportive, have an abundant and positive attitude, are trustworthy, and think like me. According to motivational speaker Jim Rohn, you are the composite of the five people you spend the most time with. Think about your family, friends, and co-workers, and ask yourself: "Who are those five people today?"

If you are clear about what you need from your tribe, then you will be certain when you find it. So, where do you start looking? Does anyone close to you possess the qualities you are looking for? Find a friend who has similar financial interests to yours, and check in with each other regularly.

Is there a local women's group that offers workshops or meetings? Start your own Women's Money Circle. Call in the troops. Put your intentions out there and have people find you. Facebook, social media. There is a strong power gained when women collaborate with other women. Not only can you inspire a good time, but you can flourish with support, problem solving, encouragement, and effective conversation. A circle can work even with just a few participants.

Here are some possible questions for your money circle from George Kinder, author of *Life Planning for You: How to Design and Deliver the Life of Your Dreams*.

> "Imagine that you are financially secure, that you have enough money to satisfy all of your needs, now and in the future. The question is, how would you live your life? Would you change anything? Let yourself go. Don't hold back your dreams. Would you change your life and how would you do it?
>
> "You visit your doctor who tells you that you have five to ten years left to live. The good news is that you won't ever feel sick. The bad news is that you will have no notice of the moment of your death. What will you do in the time you have remaining to live? Your finances remain as they currently stand. Will you change your life, and how would you do it?
>
> "This time, your doctor shocks you with the news that you have only one day left to live. Notice what feelings arise as you confront your very real mortality. Reflecting on your life, both all your accomplishments to date and all the things that you will leave unfinished or undone, ask yourself: What did I miss? Who did I not get to be? What did I not get to do?"

These are the signature questions in the Kinder Institute of Life Planning's training program to become a Registered Life Planner®.[14]

Can you start a book club? Remember in chapter six when I asked you to refer to your own money story, experiences, and dreams? In your book club, use this chapter to spark conversation and ask your participants to share their answers. On our passage to financial empowerment, we need a call to action to talk about money more. The solution to overcoming our money worries and fears is to tackle them head on. Use a book club to master your money.

Barbara Stanny wrote in her book, *Prince Charming Isn't Coming: How Women Get Smart about Money*, "Something happens when a woman becomes financially responsible. She becomes powerful. She has the means to effect change, to really make a difference, in areas of life that matter to her most. And when an economically independent woman joins with other smart women, they wield tremendous social, economic and political clout. Together, women can become the driving force that will actually transform the world and ultimately heal the planet."

Your tribe is waiting. However, the path to find it can only be blazed by you!

I have shared my stories and guidance with you so that you can participate in this journey of mastering your money to align with your heart and true values. My life is so different than it was that day when I curled up on the kitchen floor. Now, I am strong and confident and my sense of value has flourished, even though I am human and still have moments of doubt and fear. But it is when the doubt creeps in that I come back to everything that I have shared with you. As you live your own money story I encourage you to revisit this book often and reconnect.

If one suffers we all suffer. Togetherness is strength, power, and courage.

Author Bio

Zena started a family at age twenty-two. She had started university but then put it aside and stayed home to raise her daughters. She was broke but in love. Fast forward eight years—she was on the verge of a nervous breakdown wondering how she was going to support her two young daughters after a marriage breakdown. She chose to take the responsibility of her family's money and take control of her own destiny. At the time it felt as though her world was collapsing, but in hindsight it was just the beginning of an awareness of her personal power. She went back to university, created a career, and found a passion to help other women who find themselves wanting and needing to take control on the path to financial independence.

In 2008, she graduated from university and shortly after earned her Financial Planning designations. She has worked in financial planning since then as a Certified Financial Planner, a Certified Divorce Financial Analyst, and a Certified Cash Flow Specialist. She is the founder of Women Wine & Wealth, Regina, and of the financial planning firm, Astra Financial Services located in Regina, Saskatchewan.

Understanding family money values has been a part of her own journey to financial freedom—the freedom to stand on her own two feet again. Zena's experiences and teachings have helped to save her marriage and inspired her teenage daughters to look at money with empowerment and independence. She now inspires women to take control of their family's finances and live by the principles she teaches in this book.

[1]www.statcan.gc.ca/pub/89-503-x/2010001/article/11542-eng.htm
[2]www.prudential.com/media/managed/wm/media/Pru_Women_Study_2014.pdf?src=Newsroom&pg=WomenStudy2014
[3]www.statcan.gc.ca/pub/89-503-x/2010001/article/11441-eng.htm
[4]www.theatlantic.com/magazine/archive/2014/05/the-confidence gap/359815/
[5]Author of Couples and Money: Cracking the Code to Ending the #1 Conflict in Marriage.
[6]"Money, Sex and Happiness: An Empirical Study" by David G Blanchflower and Andrew J Oswald, www.dartmouth.edu/~blnchflr/papers/sentScanJEsexmoneyhappinessjune2003.pdf
[7]ir.yodlee.com/releasedetail.cfm?releaseid=867332
[8]Mahatma Gandhi. BrainyQuote.com, Xplore Inc, 2017. www.brainyquote.com/quotes/quotes/m/mahatmagan105593.html, accessed February 25, 2017.
[9]Stanford Experiment, www.ncbi.nlm.nih.gov/pubmed/5010404
[10]Yogi Berra. BrainyQuote.com, Xplore Inc, 2017. www.brainyquote.com/quotes/quotes/y/yogiberra391900.html, accessed February 25, 2017.
[11]With permission
[12]Read more about these principles in How to Be a Pink Flamingo in a Brown Duck Pond.
[13]Tribes: We Need You to Lead Us, page 1, used with permission.
[14]They are used by permission of George Kinder and the Kinder Institute of Life Planning, © Copyright 1999. All Rights Reserved.

More About Zena

Zena Amundsen is a certified financial planner, certified divorce financial analyst and a certified cashflow specialist. Her experience and education match her passion.

Personal Finance is a topic that doesn't need to be boring, or product/sales related. Money affects everyone. Let's talk more about it, our behaviours and how to gain a sense of confidence around our money. Zena Amundsen has a passion for educating individuals on financial topics. She has participated and contributed to the website Advisor.ca which is a go-to resource for Canadian advisors and the Globe and Mail -Globe Advisor.

You can also find Zena supporting women with Women Wine & Wealth Regina and supporting the Regina YMCA as a Heritage Committee board member.

Zena Amundsen is founder and owner of Astra Financial Services, a Financial Planning firm in Regina, Saskatchewan. Contact her at www.astrafinancial.ca

You can book her to speak at your workplace, event, radio interview and media appearance.

zena@astrafinancial.ca

www.ingramcontent.com/pod-product-compliance
Lightning Source LLC
Chambersburg PA
CBHW060449240326
41598CB00088B/4307

9780995966604